BUSINESS MATTERS FOR WOMEN

Joyce O'Connor

and

Helen Ruddle

Attic Press

Dublin

First Published in 1990 by
Attic Press
44 East Essex Street
Dublin 2

British Library Cataloguing in Publication Data
O'Connor, Joyce
    Business matters for women handbook.
    1. Business enterprise. Success
    I. Title II. Ruddle, Helen
    650.1

    ISBN 0-946211-87-6

Cover Design: Concept: Brenda McArdle
Origination: Attic Press
Printed and bound in Great Britain
The Guernsey Press Co. Ltd., Guernsey, Channel Islands.

Acknowledgements

We would like to thank all those who by contributing their experiences, ideas and feedback made this book possible. We are very grateful to the many women who took time off from running their businesses to tell us what life is like for women in the business world and whose experiences form the basis of this book. Marion Deegan of Shannon Development and Eileen Banks of the IDA also gave generously of their time to read the original draft and give us their comments and observations. We would also like to thank Dr Tony Humphreys for several helpful discussions and many productive ideas. Valuable feedback and comments were given by Pat O'Connor and our publishers, Attic Press.

Thanks are also due to Teresa Curry and Christine Langan for their skill, patience and good humour in processing this manuscript.

Contents

Introduction

Business Matters for Women

Nowadays the business world is no longer the exclusive province of men as more and more women are taking up the option of self-employment and setting up businesses themselves. Have you ever thought about starting up in business? If you have, then this book is for you.

This is an exciting time for women now that the changing nature of work is beginning to open up new opportunities and challenges. In particular, it is emerging that business really does matter for women. Business is becoming a real career option for women and an important means of self-advancement, fulfilment and economic independence. Increasingly, business is being seen as a possible solution to problems arising from unemployment, redundancy, emigration or attempts to return to work after raising a family. Many women too see business as a more attractive work alternative than attempting to overcome barriers to advancement in traditional organisations. In the USA, for example, women are going into business for themselves at twice the rate of men. In Ireland too, despite the unemployment statistics, and the gloomy headlines on recession, there are many opportunities for new businesses. Many women are exploiting this potential with women-owned businesses being the fastest growing sector, particularly in the service area.

The entrepreneurial spirit is not new for women. Down through the years women have been involved in small-scale enterprises. Women have often been the silent partners with their spouses in running a small business or a farm enterprise. Nowadays, however, women are taking a more public and prominent role in the world of business. These women entrepreneurs are not superwomen different from the ordinary community of women. They are women like yourself and you too can join them.

The advice from successful Irish business women is that if you have a good idea for a business you should just go ahead and do it. It is important to have a positive approach and a positive self-image and to believe in your ability to be successful. Most importantly, these women emphasise that the business idea is vital, that you must know what you are setting out to do, be well-prepared, have done your homework and, above all else, you must plan. The key to success is realism and 'intelligent planned anticipation'.

Do I want to be in business?

This book is about giving you the practical information you need to help you through start-up and the growth and development of your business. Before getting started on practical plans, however, it is well to consider whether setting-up in business is really the best option for you. Running a business can be a struggle and can involve a huge amount of work and you need to be highly motivated and committed. The first part of the book is designed to help you answer the question 'Do I Want To Be in Business?' and guides you in thinking about your particular interests, abilities, motivations and skills. This kind of self-assessment enables you to consider the options open to you and to make your choices on a sound, well thought-out basis. Motivation on its own, however, is not enough. Identifying a feasible idea is essential and you must also have practical information and know-how.

How do I get started?

If you have decided that the business world is for you then the next question is 'How Do I Get Started?'. Looking ahead, making plans and preparing the groundwork thoroughly will all ensure that your business gets off to a good start. The second part of the book provides practical advice on what you need to know; on where to go for information; and on agencies that will help you. There is practical guidance on preparing a feasible business plan and on realistic goal-setting.

What is involved in running a business?

The third section looks at the question of what is involved in running a business once past the initial start-up decision. How do you manage marketing? What does financial management involve? What is involved in the management of production? If you employ others, what management issues are involved here? You will find information which will help you to deal with these questions and ensure that your business not only survives beyond the start-up stage but will also, if you decide, grow and develop. This part of the book describes the kinds of management issues you are likely to face and indicates means of dealing with them which may be useful.

What about my home and personal life?

The focus of the final part of the book is on how to look after yourself as well as run a successful business. How do you manage your time so that home, personal and social life are not neglected? How do you deal with stress? How do you make time for leisure activities? Guidelines are provided which will help ensure that your work life is successful without cost to your personal and social life.

Business Matters For Women is not a text-book on how to start up a business or on business management skills. It is intended to familiarise you with the essential requirements of running a business, to provide you with a strong base of information and to give you a practical understanding of the area. The book is aimed both at the woman who is just thinking about setting up in business and also at those women already in business and those considering growth and expansion. Its chief aim is to:

* provide practical guidelines on how to set about starting up in business.

* increase your awareness of the problems likely to arise so that you can anticipate and prepare for them before you start.

* provide guidelines on running the business once up-and going.

* provide guidelines on effective management of growth and expansion.

* outline the steps involved so that you can approach setting up and running a business in an organised way.

* raise questions you will need to ask yourself at different stages of business development and indicate how you can set about finding the answers.

* point you towards sources of help and advice.

Chapter One

Is the business world for you? The business decision

Whatever your background, whatever your educational achievements, whatever your age, you too can start up and run a successful business provided you plan and prepare properly. However, before getting started, it is important to take a step back and to critically consider what you want from life and whether business can help you achieve what you want. You need to do some careful personal examination and stock-taking before you begin.

The success of the venture will revolve to a very great extent around you and your motivation, commitment, capabilities and strengths. You will be responsible for its development and management and for whatever risks and rewards there are. Running a business involves much hard work and effort and may mean a major commitment such as leaving your job, investing any savings you may have, working long hours and borrowing money. At the very beginning then it is important to ask yourself if you have the motivation and commitment and if the business world is really for you. Getting to know yourself, being aware of your strengths and limitations, is the first step on the road to a successful business start-up.

Questions to think about. Write down your answers.

* Have you drive and energy?

* Are you the kind of person who looks for solutions rather than focusing on problems?

* How would you rate your level of motivation?

* Would you be prepared to invest any savings you have in the business?

* How committed are you to setting up in business?

---

* Are you prepared to give it top priority in terms of time and effort over the start-up period?

* How good is your health?

* If you are currently in a job, how would you feel about giving it up to devote yourself full-time to the business?

* Are you prepared for hard work and long hours?

* Are you determined and willing to fight for what you want?

Why do you want to set up in business?

Think too about your reasons for setting up in business. What do you hope to get out of this venture? Below are some of the best things that Irish women entrepreneurs say they get out of being in business. Do these apply to you?

	Yes	No
* independence		
* freedom to plan your time as you want		
* being your own boss; being in the driver's seat		
* financial reward		
* delight and satisfaction in producing a high-quality product		
* self-fulfilment		
* the 'sweet smell of success'		
* opportunities for meeting people		

What are your hopes and aspirations? What do you want out of life?

Will being in business help you to achieve your hopes and aspirations?

What are your personal strengths and shortcomings?

Running a business is not for everyone. It takes certain skills and personal qualities such as those described below. It is not essential that you possess all of these skills and qualities. You can always compensate for shortcomings or remedy them as long as you identify and acknowledge them. Use the questionnaire below to think through your strengths and shortcomings.

Personal qualities

Does this apply to you?	Yes	No
Need for Control and Independence Do you like to be in situations where the outcome is influenced by your own ability rather than by luck or chance? Do you believe that your success depends on yourself rather than forces outside yourself? Do you like to be in control of decisions in your workplace?		
Drive and Energy Would you describe yourself as a doer? Do you organise and plan your time?		
Self-Confidence Do you see yourself as having a positive self-image? Would you describe yourself as self-confident?		
Skill in problem-solving Do you follow through on things? When confronted with a problem do you see a range of possible solutions? Do you look for help with difficult problems?		
Skill in Goal or Target Setting Do you set clear-cut goals for yourself? Can you work towards targets that may seem far in the future?		
Calculated Risk Taking Are you realistic in recognising what you can do? How important are job security and permanency to you? As a risk-taker do you like a sure thing? Are you careful or a gambler?		
Ability to Deal with Failure Do you get discouraged by setbacks? Or do you look on mistakes as a learning opportunity?		

Does this apply to you?	Yes	No
Use of Feedback Do you look on feedback as a means of improving performance? Or does negative feedback make you feel defensive or downhearted? Do you actively seek out feedback?		
Ability to Take Initiative Do you actively seek responsibility in a work situation? Do you like to take the initiative in situations? Do you like to be responsible for the success or failure of a project you undertake?		
Tolerance of Ambiguity and Uncertainty How do you deal with a situation where there is uncertainty or insecurity?		

Having thought about the qualities above, list:

Your Strengths

Your Shortcomings

What help do you need?

What are you going to do about your shortcomings?

Would involving others in a business team make up for some of the shortcomings you have identified?

Build on your experience

Successful business women advise that you start with what you know best and build on that knowledge. It will help your business greatly if you start up in an area where you have had previous experience. For one young woman, the answer to what business she should start came from her family background. Her parents had a duck farm and while growing up she had gained a lot of knowledge and experience in the business of producing fowl. However, rather than produce ducks, chickens or turkeys which were already being widely produced, she decided to breed quails. She had already visited a producer of quails in England, saw what was involved and had seen evidence that her idea could work. This is not to suggest that you cannot start-up in a field where you have had no previous experience. If you start-up with partners who know the field or if you buy a franchise, then previous experience is less important.

If you have previously worked outside the home or are presently in a paid job, ask yourself what skills you have acquired here which you can use in running your business. Have you experience of, for example, taking responsibility, of making decisions, of taking initiative? Have you had to supervise the work of others, to motivate them, to reward them for work well done and confront them when difficulties arise?

Don't be discouraged if you have never worked outside the home, or not for a long period. Within the home you will almost certainly have developed skills which translate very well to the world of business - skills, for example, in decision-making, in seeking out sources of information, in organising activities, in planning ahead. Think also about your hobbies and leisure activities as these will also have enabled you to develop a variety of skills.

Using the following headings, jot down all the strengths, talents and skills you have acquired at this stage of your life.

My Talents and Skills

Work-related skills   For example, computer programming, marketing, accounting, organisation and planning of work, delegation of work.

Skills developed in the home For example, budgeting, time management, dealing with interpersonal relations.

Skills related to hobbies and interests For example, attentiveness to detail, perseverance, manual dexterity, good hand-eye co-ordination.

Skills developed through voluntary activities For example, organisation skills, dealing with people, accounting, public speaking.	
Personal qualities For example, determination, flexibility, creativity, clear-thinker, assertive.	
Communication skills For example, ability to write well, knowledge of a foreign language, good at marshalling your thoughts, able to ask for what you want in a direct fashion.	
Interpersonal skills For example, good at motivating others, ability to deal with confrontation, able to express feelings, openness, tolerance.	

Responsibilities and obligations

Running a business involves certain pressures and demands and these will need to be balanced against the roles and responsibilities currently in your life. Everyone has relationships in their lives that are important to them and that demand commitment. You will need to think how being in business is going to affect these relationships. You will also need to think about practical considerations and to ask yourself questions such as these:

What I Plan to Do	
Is your business to be a part-time or full-time effort?	
How will being in business affect your personal and social life?	
If you have children, how will home and childcare arrangements be worked out?	
If you currently have a job with benefits such as a pension scheme, health insurance, or company car, how will you manage without these?	
Have you enough money to tide you over should you fall ill?	

Are you prepared to take a drop in your standard of living while your business gets off the ground? Would you be willing to sell some of your possessions to raise money to start up?	

It is important to consider how you will cope with these pressures and demands. Think about the personal resources you can draw on. Where are your shortcomings and what help can you get from others in making up for these shortcomings? It can be useful to talk to other women in business about the demands and pressures they have experienced and the means of coping they have developed and used. Think through the lifestyle implications of being in business.

What factors are in your favour?

Apart from your personal qualities and skills and your motivation and commitment, there are three further factors which will very much influence your chances of success in business. Ask yourself the following questions:

Level of experience What kind of business experience have you? Is it, for example, limited to selling? Have you managerial experience? Is your experience in office administration? Have you previous experience in your chosen field of business? Perhaps you know very little about the particular area. Perhaps your experience is limited or short-term, maybe you have long experience in the field. What about your financial situation. Do you have any money or access to finance? Are your resources limited; reasonably secure; sufficient for a year; no problem?	

Training

Running a business requires certain types of expertise - for example, in marketing, in finance, in production, in dealing with personnel. Do not be disheartened if you do not possess all these skills at the outset. Nobody is good at everything. So, if you are aware of areas where you lack business skills, rather than complaining about it, set about acquiring the kinds of skills you will need, or think about how you can compensate for shortcomings.

High level expertise is more important in some businesses than in others. If you find that it is vital in the business you are planning and you are not an expert and do not have the time or opportunity to acquire the expertise, you will need to consider carefully the costs involved in hiring staff or in paying consultants to provide the skills needed. Use state agencies such as FAS or the IDA for advice. A list of resources is given at the end of the book. Perhaps you know someone who has the skills you lack and who would be willing to be your partner in the business?

Think too about training possibilities. There is a wide range of courses available for people starting up in business. FAS and some Vocational Education Committees (VEC) run courses on how to start your own business. A specific course for women has been developed by FAS called the 'Women Into Enterprise Programme'. If you have already started up in business, FAS offers several training opportunities for developing different kinds of business management skills in areas such as finance, marketing and sales and production. Apart from state agency training opportunities, which are free, there are also other avenues to the development of business management skills through different types of degree or diploma courses in different institutions (listed at the end of the book). Development Agencies such as the IDA and Shannon Development and some financial institutions also often run special seminars geared towards setting up in business.

Using professional advisors

Successful business people are never shy of seeking advice and become quite expert at using whatever resources are around. Much advice is freely available from a variety of state agencies but you may also need to hire advisors. Many small businesses are reluctant to think about hiring professional advisors because of the expected high cost. You should, however, balance the cost involved against the potential savings in the future as mistakes can be costly.

The amount of outside professional advice you need depends, of course, on your own expertise and experience, and on that of your employees (if you have others working with you). There are, however, certain advisors whom you almost certainly will need at some time in the course of you business - for example, banker, solicitor, accountant and insurance agent. Shop around when seeking outside professional advice. Ask other business women whom they would recommend. As a general rule, look for people who have experience in your particular line of business.

Remember

Your personal stock-taking may have led you to conclude that you have many of the skills and qualities of a successful business person. However, you need to remember that having the 'correct' personality profile does not guarantee business success. You also need practical information and know-how. On the other hand, it is important that you should not be discouraged if you do not appear to fully measure up to what seems to be required. There are many examples of people who, on the surface at least, do not seem like likely candidates for a business career and yet have achieved outstanding success. Remember the advice given by business women who have succeeded in setting up in business - **go out and do it!**

Chapter Two

Getting the right idea

Getting the right idea for a service or product is clearly a vital first step in setting up a business. It is well to remember, however, that an idea alone does not create a successful business. A clever business idea will get you nowhere unless there is a market for your product or service and unless you have the skills to exploit that market. The successful business person focuses on a combination of market, idea and money.

You may already know what kind of business you want to set up and, if so, the main issues for you are how to get started and where to begin. On the other hand, you may be at the stage where you know you would like to be in business but have not yet got a definite business idea. Despite the popular notion of the sudden flash of inspiration that leads to the brilliant business idea, more often than not getting the right idea is the result of a lot of hard thinking and deliberate search. Ideas rarely occur by accident or coincidence. If you sit around waiting for the idea to come, nothing will happen. You need to seek out and explore ideas and this may take considerable time and resources. Where do entrepreneurs get their ideas for business? How do they identify opportunities? Successful business people say that they identify opportunities and get their ideas from a variety of sources.

*   previous work situation
*   hobbies and leisure activities
*   domestic and personal experience
*   business contacts
*   unique knowledge of a particular market area
*   state agencies
*   experience in voluntary work.

For one Irish business woman, her business idea developed out of the frustration she experienced in attempting to find Irish made products for her children. This woman started with the notion of producing Easter eggs. Using her own children as her market audience she came up with the idea of using a popular character on Irish Children's television to sell the product. She clarified the copyright situation, went ahead and the combination of Easter egg in a mug featuring the TV character proved to be a winner.

Strategies for finding ideas

* What are you good at? Do you have particular skills that could be used as the basis for a business?

* If you are currently employed or have previously worked, is there anything you are doing that suggests an idea for a business?

* Think about your personal life and homecare tasks. Is there some product you could make that would make some task easier? Is there some service that would be useful?

* Is there some gap in the market that you have spotted and could supply?

* Maybe you have come across some product while on holidays abroad that you feel would sell in this country.

* Look at books and magazines - are there any ideas there that you could use?

* Take note of the things people complain about. Maybe you can produce a product that solves the problem or functions more efficiently.

* Is there some item or service that you have had difficulty in finding - could you provide this yourself?

* When shopping, notice items that are being imported into the country. Check import lists. Could you produce any of these items?

---

*   If you can, visit trade fairs and exhibitions in the areas that interest you. This is an excellent way of seeing the products of potential competitors and of finding out about product and market trends.

*   Perhaps you can find a new and more efficient way of marketing an existing product or service?

*   If you have the germ of an idea and can identify potential customers, perhaps you can meet with them and find out what their needs are and where existing products or services fall short.

*   If you have contacts with distributors or wholesalers who distribute the kind of product you are interested in, they may be able to give you useful feedback on the shortcomings of existing products and the kinds of improvements customers would like.

A brainstorming session is a very useful means of coming up with ideas. In brainstorming you just let all the ideas flow, no matter how daft or far-fetched they may seem. Evaluation comes at a later stage when all ideas have been aired. Because literally anything goes, brainstorming allows people to be as creative as possible. The other advantage is that hearing one person's idea often touches off other ideas.

State agencies can also be of help to you in identifying a manufacturing business opportunity. Pay a visit to one of the Small Business Information Centres attached to the regional offices or the head office of the Industrial Development Authority (IDA). If you are in Dublin, call to the IDA's Walk-In centre. You can also commission the state agency, EOLAS, or other private commercial agencies to carry out a special 'product search' for you in the area in which you are interested. The search will shortlist a number of possible products based on a study of trade literature, exhibitions, licensing journals and so on. There may be a fee involved so check before you ask to have the search done.

Remember

You do not have to come up with a completely new idea. Many successful businesses are founded on, for example, improving an existing product or service or on substituting a home-produced for an imported product.

Often it is the most obvious idea that has the greatest potential. Well-known examples are all around: The Sock Shop, Budget Travel, The Body Shop. Many business women have used their home base as a launching pad for their ideas. However, while the traditional areas of women's expertise, such as arts and crafts, clothing and food are a rich source of business ideas, Irish women are now beginning to move into non-traditional high-technology type enterprises, such as the development of computer software. So keep your horizons broad and do not be restricted by stereotyped ideas of 'appropriate' business areas for women.

Testing out your idea

You may think you have come up with a brilliant idea but it is important to check whether others agree.

---

* Keep a record of all your ideas and then draw up a shortlist which you belive is worth following up.

  Shortlist

* Discuss your ideas with your advisors or with friends and use their feedback to assess the viability of the opportunities you have identified.

  Feedback

* What do you think of your idea yourself? What are its strong points? What are its shortcomings? What can you do about its shortcomings?

  Strong points

  Shortcomings

  Improvements

* Think about your expertise, skills and experience and whether these are appropriate for putting your idea into action.

  What have you learned?

* Consider whether you have any financial resources to help you follow through on your idea.

  What financial resources can you draw on?

While discussing your idea with others can be a very useful source of feedback on its viability, it is worth keeping in mind that others may not always share your enterprising spirit and willingness to take a calculated risk. If there is opposition to your idea you need to sort out how much is genuinely related to the viability of your proposal and how much is a reflection of the other person's own attitudes and viewpoint. Beware begrudgers. Discussing your idea with other business women who have had personal experience of the start-up process can give you a valuable indication of how realistic your proposal is likely to be.

Getting help

One of the most important ingredients for success in business is the ability to access and use all the sources of information and help available to you - written sources, other people, organisations. The successful business woman will learn from everyone and every situation. Use public libraries. Discuss issues with other business women. Use your work situation, your home situation, your informal network of contacts - all these are useful sources of information. If you are not currently working you may not have an extensive network of contacts and, for you, formal sources of information are particularly important. There is a whole range of state agencies which will help you in testing the viability of your business idea. For example:

* The Industrial Development Authority (IDA)
* Shannon Development Company Ltd
* Udarás na Gaeltachta
* The Irish Goods Council
* The Innovation Centre, Limerick
* Dublin Innovation Centre
* South West Business Innovation Centre, Cork
* Galway Business Innovation Centre
* EOLAS (The Irish Science and Technology Agency)
* FAS
* CTT (Irish Export Board)
* The Bolton Trust Dublin.

Getting the most out of state agencies

State agencies devote considerable resources to helping people set up in business. These resources include:

* advice
* information
* library facilities
* free reading material
* displays and exhibitions
* training programmes
* financial aid.

Find out from these agencies what help they are offering that may be useful to you at this stage. When you start asking you may be surprised at the amount of help that is available. The IDA, Shannon Development, Udarás na Gaeltachta, for example, provide Feasibility Study Grants which repay some of the cost of finding out whether a particular idea is viable. You may want to check out the 'product development' service offered by EOLAS whereby the agency sets up a production model for producing the goods you have in mind. The Innovation Centre in Limerick rents out Business Incubation Units which provide all the office services needed to research and develop a business idea. People exploring a business idea rent the units as a working base on a month-to-month basis. Fees vary depending on whether the business involved is in manufacturing or international services or in some other area. Advice on the use of microelectronics in new products or manufacturing processes is available from, for example, the Microelectronics Applications Centre (MAC) attached to the University of Limerick, from EOLAS in Dublin and the National Microelectronics Research Centre in University College, Cork. It is up to you to exploit the assistance that is available. Identify and accept your own need for assistance; remember that help is there and go after it. Knock on all doors and ask for what you need.

You should keep the following points in mind when approaching agencies for assistance:

---

* It is unwise to have unrealistic expectations of what agencies can do for you. Their function is to advise and facilitate you but they cannot do the work for you. You are the one who has to set up the business.

---

* Before visiting agencies get their literature first by post.
* Think about your information needs beforehand and the questions you want to ask.

  Information Needs List

* Contacts are very useful. Get the name of someone specific if possible.

  Contact

* Ask all the questions you need to ask - however small or naive they may seem to you. You will avoid much frustration and problems at a later stage if you make sure now that you fully understand the information you are being given.

* Remember that you may not always see the same person when you visit an agency. Some women starting up in business have said they found it difficult not having a one-to-one relationship with an agency member at the beginning. Rather than being disappointed if this does not happen for you, turn it to your advantage and use it as an opportunity to get different points of view.

* Be prepared for the fact that initially, as a woman, you may not be taken seriously as a business person. How you present yourself is very important here. The issue for you is to get across your sense of purpose, your ability, your determination and your confidence in yourself and your idea. Keep in mind how you want to be viewed and behave accordingly.

* If you do meet with a less than enthusiastic response to your business idea, probe for the underlying reasons for this. Ask questions: for example, what seems to be the main problem? Address their problem and ask them for feedback. What is the key issue here - is it the idea, my abilities, the potential market? What do you advise me to do? It would be foolish to refuse to look at all negative feedback but neither do you have to accept it unquestioningly.

* Beware of getting wrong or conflicting advice.

Networking

Because women are comparatively new to the world of business in significant numbers and because many women entrepreneurs come from the home rather than the work sphere, they often do not have access to the same network of contacts as men. In order to provide support for each other and to provide a means of sharing experiences and knowledge, a Network for Women in Business has been formed in Ireland. There is also another group called Network for Women in the Professions and in Business and a Network for Women in Local Employment Initiatives. Contact with these groups can help you boost your confidence if you are anxious or unsure about starting up your own business. Addresses are listed at the end of the book. Use the Network Directory of Women-owned Businesses to help you expand your network of contacts in the business world. Talk to your friends. They will be interested and may very well be able to help. But do beware of giving away too much information to a competitor or potential competitor.

Chapter Three

Getting started

Having the idea for a business is one thing but putting the idea into action is quite another thing altogether. Not knowing where to start, you may feel daunted by the prospect of attempting to turn your idea into reality. Remember that businesses grow and develop through a series of stages:

* pre-start-up
* start-up
* teething problems
* consolidation
* survival
* success
* growth.

Getting to the stage where the business is up and running is preceded by an initial stage of exploration and planning. This is where you start and you are more likely to be successful if you do not rush this stage in your zeal to get the venture going. A major cause of failure among young businesses is lack of planning. The best way to increase your chances of success is to plan thoroughly and then follow through your plans. The start-up phase is often the most difficult for women entrepreneurs. Business women say, however, that once past the start-up obstacles, running a business is no more difficult for women than it is for men. Once established, the key issues are business-related rather than gender-related.

What type of business do you want?

There are many different options within the business world and you need to consider at the outset which option best suits you. Different types of business have different requirements and you are more likely to be successful if you choose the kind of business whose requirements match the skills and qualities you have to offer. These are the main business options:

* *Manufacturing* where you are actually making something. The product may be anything from computer software to cheese to jewellery to toothpaste.

* *Service* where you charge a fee for performing a specific task. For example, car valeting, hairdressing, dry cleaning, photography, restaurant.

* *Professional service* For example, marketing consultant, research services, nursery school.

* *Retail - selling things* For example, bookshop, antique business, mail order business.

You may like the idea of running your own business but find it hard to come up with an idea or are anxious about your lack of experience. If so, buying a franchise could be the solution for you. Buying a franchise means that you buy the right to operate someone else's tried and tested business idea. Somebody thinks up an original business idea - for example, Bewley's Restaurant. The idea is put into practice and the business is successful. The business owner sells the right to others to start up an identical business. As a franchisee you get not only the idea but also the established name and sometimes a number of back-up services such as advertising. It is a safe way of getting started but it also has its disadvantages and it is not the cheapest way of getting a business going. There are advantages and disadvantages to all of the different business options. You need to weigh the pros and cons of each and consider how the balance works out for you personally.

What about the structure of your business?

Businesses may be structured in different ways. You can set up in business as a:

* sole trader
* partnership
* limited company
* co-operative
* local community initiative

Each type of structure has its own advantages and disadvantages. It is important to get professional advice on these before you start. For example, there may be tax advantages in one kind of structure over another. Some banks and state agencies may have difficulties in dealing with certain structures such as local community initiatives. An accountant or tax consultant can advise you on the structure that is the most efficient one for you. If raising money on your own is a problem for you, you could explore the possibility of joining with others in a co-operative or local employment initiative.

According to women who have set up as *sole traders*, the primary advantage is that power and control of the business remain solely in their hands. The sole trader structure is also easy to set up and is subject to minimal regulations. As a sole trader, however, you are personally liable for the debts of your business and should it fail your personal belongings and assets, such as your house or car, can be taken to pay your creditors.

Women involved in *partnerships* will tell you that one of the greatest advantages of this kind of business arrangement is that people's skills complement each other and individual shortcomings are thus offset. Even at the very early stages of setting up a business considerable skills in, for example, marketing and management are called upon. You may not have all these skills yourself and having a partner with complementary skills may make the difference between success and failure in guiding your venture past the initiation stage. The sharing of responsibility is also seen as a major advantage of these kinds of business structure. You can have any number of people in the partnership, some of whom may work full-time and others part-time. You may also have 'sleeping partners' who do not take an active part in the business. This kind of partner can be useful but can also cause problems such as undue interference. If you do decide to go into partnership with others it is important to have a solicitor draw up a partnership agreement which can help avoid misunderstanding or friction at a later stage. Remember that with a partnership arrangement there is unlimited liability which means that each partner is personally liable for the debts of the business and your personal belongings can be taken to pay creditors. This is another reason why you need to choose your partners carefully.

The main advantage of setting up a *limited company* is that the business is a separate legal entity from the people who manage it. Liability is limited so you are not personally liable for the debts of the business unless you have given personal guarantees or the business has operated fraudulently. However, you may find it difficult at start-up to get credit from suppliers or a bank loan unless you can give personal guarantees. Setting up a limited company is more expensive than other structures and is more complicated and subject to more regulations and formalities. For example, you must be registered with the Registrar of Companies, you must appoint an auditor and your annual audited accounts must be sent to the Registrar - all of this can be a costly exercise. There is a great deal of documentation involved including Memorandum of Association, Articles of Association, Minute Book, Company Seal and Certificate of Incorporation. If you are setting up a limited company it is most important that you get professional advice from a solicitor or accountant.

With the *co-operative structure*, every member has an equal voice in decision-making and is entitled to share in the profits but is also responsible for losses. The primary advantages of this structure are the support, shared responsibility and friendship which typically develop. The members of a co-operative are protected by limited liability just as in a limited company. Co-operatives are eligible for all IDA grants for manufacturing businesses. However, unlike limited companies, they do not have the benefit of the reduced tax rate of 10% on manufacturing profits. You may, of course, change the structure of your business as it grows and develops. You may, for example, start out as a sole trader or partnership and later, as your business expands, decide to form a limited company. Whatever type of business you set up, if you adopt a business name other than your own name you must register it with the Registrar of Business Names. The Registrar will be able to tell you if the name you have chosen is already being used by another business. Remember that this service will cost you money.

Building a business team

Studies of business women show that while partnership arrangements sometimes arise spontaneously from a woman's existing relationships, the more successful arrangements are those where the partners are chosen deliberately for the particular skills they possess. Business women also say that it is important that you choose a partner whose personality is compatible with yours and with other people in the business arrangement.

What is important here is that you do some critical analysis at the outset. As outlined in the first chapter, the first step is self-assessment, where you take a critical look at your own:

*   motivation
*   business expertise
*   managerial skills

* expectations
* team skills
* responsibilities and demands on you

Your second step is to analyse your business. Here you look at:

* what business you are going to be in
* what are your major goals for the business
* what needs to be done to realise those goals
* what factors are critical to the success of your business
* what special skills and expertise are needed
* what external resources are required

Having done your self-assessment and taken a critical look at your business, your next step is to assess how well your motivation, capabilities and expertise match the requirements of your venture. You now need to ask yourself:

* where are the gaps between what I have to offer and what the business needs?
* how do I make good these shortcomings?
* should I employ others to offset these shortcomings?
* can I afford to employ them?
* would part-time assistance be enough?
* could colleagues supply the needed expertise?
* do I need professional assistance?
* when do I need the additional expertise?

In choosing people to form a business team, it is important to do it systematically, not in a haphazard fashion where, for example, you say to yourself: 'I know Joan, she seems a capable sort of person, maybe I'll ask her to join the team.' If the team is to work out satisfactorily there must be:

* matching of skills and abilities
* trust between members
* shared expectations
* commitment to the team and business
* compatibility

Remember that selection of the business team members is only the first phase. Building the team so that it works together cohesively as a group will take time and effort and commitment.

Starting-Up

A very important step in getting started is to draw up your business plan. This plan is a very important document for a number of reasons, not least of which is its influence in helping you raise money. Both of these aspects of getting started - the business plan and raising finance - are discussed in the following two chapters.

Chapter Four

Preparing a business plan

Your business plan is a very important document and drawing it up is a crucial step in getting your business idea off the ground. From the point of view of financial institutions, your business plan is essential in providing them with the information they need to assess the viability of your proposed venture. If you do not have a plan, you will find that people will be very reluctant to back you. If you want to be taken seriously, you must show that you have done your homework, that you know what you are talking about, that you have given the idea much thought and have planned ahead. State agencies you may be dealing with at this stage do not always require a plan but having it will show you mean business. Planning your business right from the start is one of the main keys to success. The advantages to yourself of drawing up a business plan are that it:

* helps you to understand where you are and how to get where you want to be

* encourages you to discipline your thinking and forces you to take an objective, critical look at your venture

* enables you to think through methodically the steps you need to take

* provides a framework for making decisions and planning strategies over the coming years

* makes you aware of potential pitfalls and forces you to think of means of overcoming them

* gives you the kind of background knowledge that enables you to present your idea with confidence

* provides a benchmark against which you can review and evaluate the progress of your business.

Your plan should outline realistic expectations and the long term goals of your business. It should highlight strengths and anticipate concerns about weaknesses. It is best to confront the positive and negative aspects of the business head-on and to discuss them explicitly.

It can pay to get external help and guidance in preparing your plan. State agencies such as the IDA and also banks provide guidelines and valuable assistance. Perhaps you can go to one of the 'start your own business' courses run by FAS. it is important, however, that you are involved in the development of your plan and that you understand it - it must be *your* plan and not your advisors'. A typical business plan covers the following main areas:

* Cover and Title page.
* Table of Contents.
* Brief introduction outlining the background, purpose and format of the plan.
* Separate sections on describing the business; market analysis and marketing; manufacturing or operations; management; financial data.
* Conclusion.
* Appendices containing tables and supporting documents such as your CV, financial projections, market statistics.

The plan should be typed double-spaced on one side and the pages should be numbered and bound. Make it as clear and concise as possible.

The checklist below will take you through the steps needed to draw up your plan. The following chapters discuss in greater detail different aspects of business outlined in the plan. Some of the items in the checklist will be more relevant to some types of business than to others. Tailor the guidelines to suit your individual circumstances.

Cover and Title Page

Give the name of the business, your name, address and phone number (if you have one) along with the date.

Table of Contents

List the different chapters and the subheadings within chapters along with their appropriate page numbers.

Introduction

Describe the business briefly and its background. Outline the purpose of the plan. Indicate the format and lay-out of the plan.

Personal Profile

Briefly outline your qualifications and skills, any business or managerial experience you may have and any business-related work experience. Provide a similar account for any partners in the business.

Summary

After you have completed your business plan, go back over it and draw up a summary of the key points. Insert this summary - about one page in length - before the detailed plan begins. Include for example:

* the present status of the business
* product or service being offered
* profile of market, marketing strategies, sales plan and competitive position
* benefits to customers of product or service
* summary of financial situation and 3-5 year financial projections
* objectives over 3-5 years and action plan for reaching objectives
* strengths and shortcomings
* assessment of risk
* funding required to meet objectives

Business profile

The purpose of this section is to provide the background against which the reader of the plan can view the detailed information presented in following sections on the product and its market. This section should describe the following aspects of your business:

* Background, origins and present status.
* Company structure.
* Product or service being offered. Describe these in detail and how they are to be used. Highlight any unique features and any differences to what is currently on the market. Describe the present state of development of the product or service. Describe any patent or copyright features. Discuss any opportunities for expansion or development.
* Industry in which business will operate. Outline the current status and prospects. Discuss trends and factors that could affect the industry.
* Objectives of the business, both short-term and long-term.
* Plans for reaching objectives.
* Management.

Market analysis

The purpose of this section is to show that your proposed product or service has a market and can achieve sales in the face of competition. It is one of the most important parts of your plan. It is known that a major turn-off to financiers is the plan which focuses too heavily on the product or service at the expense of focusing on the needs and preferences of potential customers. This section of your plan should cover questions such as the following:

* Is there a demand for your product or service?
* Why should customers buy your product or service?
* Who are your potential customers? What are their characteristics and preferences? Where are they located?
* What is your target segment - is it up-market, middle-of-the-road, popular appeal? Is it a home or export market or a combination of both?
* What size is your market in terms of sales volume and sales value?
* Is the market growing, stable or declining?
* what is the growth potential of the market?
* What share of the market do you think you will get now and in 3-5 years time?
* What are the future trends in the market?
* Who are your competitors? How large is the competition? What are their strategies?
* Why should people buy from you rather than from your competitors? How do you compare with competitors in terms of price, quality, service, range of choice, delivery?

Marketing plan

This part of your plan should outline your overall marketing strategy, sales and service policies, pricing, distribution and advertising strategies.

* How will potential customers be identified? How will they be contacted?
* What features of your product or service will you emphasise to promote sales, quality, price or delivery?

* Will your product or service be introduced on a regional or national basis?
* What price will you charge for your product or service? How does your price compare with your competitors?
* What is your gross profit margin?
* What is the relationship between price, market share and profit?
* If your price is to be lower than your competitors, explain how you can do this and still be profitable.
* If your price is higher than competitors, justify this increase.
* Will you sell direct or wholesale?
* What are your channels of distribution?
* How and where are you going to promote your product or service?
* How much will promotion cost?
* How will you break into the market?

Manufacturing and operations

This part of your plan should describe the kind of facilities, location, equipment and labour force required to provide your product or service.

* Give address and physical features of the business building. Indicate whether building is rented or owned by you, whether any renovations are needed and how much they cost. Discuss any advantages and disadvantages of the location in terms, for example, of availability of labour, access to transport and closeness to customers.
* Describe plant space, storage, machinery and other capital equipment.
* Will equipment be leased or bought, new or second-hand? How much will it cost?
* Describe the manufacturing processes involved in producing your goods.
* Will any sub-contracting be involved?
* Describe how you plan to approach quality control, production control, inventory control. What procedures will you use to minimise service problems and customer dissatisfaction?

Management

* What are the key management roles and who will fill them?
* What are to be the duties and responsibilities of people in management positions?
* What are the strengths and shortcomings? How are shortcomings to be overcome?
* Describe advice and assistance available from professional advisors

Employment

* Outline personnel needs now and in the future. What skills are needed? Are these readily available? Is training required?
* Describe employees' hours and whether they are to work part-time or full-time.

Finance

This part of your plan should indicate the potential of your business and the estimated time-scale for financial viability.

* The three essential elements here are: Profit and Loss Forecast for three years; Cash Flow Projections for three years and Balance Sheets at start-up, half-yearly in the first year and at the end of the first three years of operation. These three aspects of finance are discussed fully in the following chapter.
* From your cash flow projections indicate how much finance is required.
* How much finance is to be raised via loans and credit?
* How much finance are you yourself contributing?
* What use is to be made of the capital raised?

Doing market research

Before you get started on setting up in business you must first be sure that your good idea actually makes good sense commercially. There is no point providing a product or service, no matter how valuable it may seem, no matter how enthusiastic you are, unless people out there want to buy it. There is a well- known saying in business that 'if you can't sell it, don't make it'. You may think that this is pretty obvious but there are endless examples where someone in business has not checked out the market and winds up with unsaleable products. The product or service you offer must not only meet some well-defined need, it must also do so in a competitive fashion. You must also ensure that there are favourable long-term prospects and that the need you are satisfying is not just a short-term fad or fashion. It is essential, then, to carry out some form of market research rather than finding yourself saying later: 'I've made this - now, who in heaven's name is going to buy it?'

If your only experience of market research is of polls in the newspapers or interviewers doing large-scale household surveys then you may think that this is a sophisticated and complicated process. However, much of what you need to know can be found in a simple and direct manner. Doing the research yourself keeps down costs and also helps you to become familiar with the field yourself and to make personal contacts. It is important, however, to do your research properly, so get advice. It may be useful to use the services of a marketing consultant or market research agency.

* Draw on your personal knowledge or work experience in the area to assess potential markets.
* Talk to people who are going to be buying your product or service.
* Read newspapers, trade magazines and published reports.
* Use your local library or the facilities of state agencies to consult trade and commercial directories.
* Write to the Central Statistics Office which can supply useful information on, for example, the population of the area where you are setting up; the age structure of the population; household composition; consumer price index; figures for imports and exports.
* See what information is available from your local Chamber of Commerce.
* Talk to people - use the information available through your network of contacts in the field.
* Visit trade fairs related to your area of business.
* Watch what your competitors are doing and how they are faring.
* Look up publications for researching product ideas available through the IDA and other state agencies.

The best means of assessing the market potential of what you are offering is to carry out some test-marketing. This involves making a prototype of your product and trying it out on a small scale with a selected sample of potential customers. Through the feedback you receive you will be able to identify problems and defects or needed improvements or modifications before you get involved in full-scale production. Remember to keep notes of the outcomes of your research efforts and write these up in a report when you have finished the task. This report will be of great value in completing your business plan and will be a critical plank in your efforts to secure a loan. Bank managers will tell you that if you apply for finance and you have not done this kind of research, you will be sent away - there is no point in making a loan application without it.

It costs time and money to check out the market thoroughly. If you are setting up a manufacturing business, check out the Feasibility Study Grants available from the IDA, Shannon Development and Udarás na Gaeltachta which can enable you to recoup some of the costs involved in an agreed market research programme.

Chapter Five

Raising finance

If, having done your market research, you are convinced of the viability of your venture, the next step is to raise the finance necessary to get your business going. Not only at start-up, but at all stages of business formation, the need for finance at a reasonable rate is a recurring theme. You should be aware that, as a woman, you may experience more difficulty in raising finance than a man in a similar business. It can happen that women are not taken seriously as business persons by financial institutions.

In addition to external barriers, women are also sometimes blocked by difficulties arising within themselves. For example, women are often unaware of the types of finance offered by different agencies and financial institutions. Often too, women entrepreneurs are reluctant to use the sources of financial support available to them. One of the biggest problems is that women, because of lack of skills and experience, sometimes lack confidence in dealing with financial matters and in dealing with financial advisors and financial institutions.

The lesson from this is to:

* Find out what you can about the different sources of financial support available.

* Ensure that you gain access to them as quickly and as efficiently as possible. The name of the game is 'advance preparation'.

* Do your homework well so that you understand what will be required of you from financial institutions before you visit them. This will give you the confidence to present yourself in a way that ensures you are taken seriously.

* Prepare your business plan thoroughly.

* Practise skills in dealing with staff of financial institutions.

* Be clear on your financial goals and make sure these are realistic.

* Get professional help where needed from a bank manager or accountant.

* Find out about training in financial skills and see if there is some course you could join.
* Show you are serious about business and that you know what you are talking about.
* Talk to other business women and get their advice and assistance.
* Build on whatever financial skills you have and on your experience so that you progressively develop your confidence.

Sources of finance

For small and medium-size businesses in general, the most usual sources of finance are:

* personal savings
* loans from family or friends
* loans from banks and other financial institutions
* equity or share capital
* tax incentives (for example, Business Expansion Scheme)
* state agency grants
* venture capital

These different sources are discussed in detail below.

Points to ponder

In thinking about using different sources of finance keep the following points in mind:

* It may be useful to get advice from an accountant or other financial expert. Remember, however, that this will involve some cost.
* Work out what your estimated costs are going to be. What are your fixed asset costs? For example, how much do you need for premises, for equipment, for fixtures and fittings, for motor vehicles? In addition to fixed asset costs, you are going to need working capital to cover the day-to-day running costs of the business.

  First-time entrepreneurs sometimes do not pay sufficient attention to their working capital needs. It is very important to think about your working capital needs from the beginning. How much are you going to need?

* Put whatever finance you have to its best use. Ensure, for example, that it is not tied up in high stocks or overdue debtors. Think about buying second-hand rather than brand-new equipment. Can you lease rather than buy premises?

* Work out the capital structure of your business - how much money are you yourself putting into the business in relation to how much is to be borrowed finance on which interest will need to be paid. The capital structure of your business will determine the extent of financial risk involved. The greater the amount of financial risk involved the more vulnerable your business is. For example, you are more vulnerable to the risk arising from difficulties related to production, management or industrial relations. You may also be in a less competitive position compared to businesses whose structure involves less financial risk

* Remember that banks are not keen to lend more than around 20% of the finance for start-up. Also, if you are in manufacturing, state agencies only contribute a percentage of the costs. You need to have at least some money of your own to invest in the business. Perhaps you have personal savings or redundancy money. Maybe you have something valuable, such as a car, which you could sell. You may consider taking out a second mortgage on your home. Or you may have family or friends who are willing, and have the money, to back you.

* If you lack the capital to start on your own but have substantial management skills and experience, you may be able to avail of a special scheme for new entrepreneurs in manufacturing businesses - the IDA Enterprise Development Scheme - to help in overcoming initial funding problems. The programme offers, for example, loan guarantees and interest subsidies on working capital loans.

* If you do not have enough money of your own to establish the right kind of capital structure, then you may want to look for an equity partner - someone who is prepared to put up risk money on a long-term basis with a view to sharing profits in the long-term. An accountant or bank manager may be able to put you in touch with local people who have money to invest.

* Investigate tax incentives, such as the Business Expansion Scheme, available to encourage people to put money into start-up or expanding manufacturing businesses and International Services. The IDA have a booklet on these: *Making The Tax System Work For You.*

* Remember that the more money you can attract into your business other than loan finance, the better. Repayment of loans and the substantial levels of interest involved will be a constant drain on your business.

* If you are setting up a limited company, consider raising share capital through outside investors.

* The last alternative is to seek loan finance from, for example, the commercial banks, finance companies, merchant banks or the Industrial Credit Corporation. Shop around and try to get the best terms you can and the longest possible term.

* The commercial banks offer different types of finance including overdrafts, term loans, leasing, letter of credit, hire purchase. Talk to your banker about what different types of finance involve and the advantages and disadvantages of each.

* If you are interested in working with others or find it difficult to raise money on your own, check out the cash incentives available for local community initiatives through the Community Enterprise Programme.

* A special grant aid programme is also available for women in local employment initiatives from the Commission of the EC as part of the Medium-Term Community Programme on Equal Opportunities for Women. Contact the Equal Opportunities Office of the EC for full information and application forms for grant-aid. The Belgian and Irish addresses are given at the end of the book.

* If you are currently unemployed, the Enterprise Allowance Scheme, administered through FAS, may be useful in opening up business possibilities for you, although the rate of weekly pay is low.

Financial assistance from state agencies

There is a whole range of financial support schemes available through state agencies. You need to familiarise yourself with these and see how you can exploit them to your best advantage. Details can be obtained from your local IDA office, Shannon Development or Udarás na Gaeltachta. Remember that cash incentives are largely directed at manufacturing businesses and international services. Check out the following:

* *Enterprise Allowance Scheme* (FAS) available to people registered as unemployed for both manufacturing and service businesses.

* *Community Enterprise Programme*   incentives for community or co-operative businesses; cash incentives and planning, development

and management grants for committed groups.

* *The Marine Credit Plan* administered through Bord Iascaigh Mhara.

* *Employment incentives and subsidies.*

* *Bord Fáilte grants* for improvements to premises, entertainment facilities and staff accommodation.

* *Training grants.*

* *Management Development grants* cash incentives and advice to help businesses develop their management capabilities.

* *Tax Relief schemes* including the Business Expansion Scheme.

* *Enterprise Development Scheme* provides loan guarantees and interest subsidies for new entrepreneurs with management skills and experience.

* *State agency financial assistance* towards establishment or expansion of manufacturing businesses including:

feasibility study grants

machinery grants

building grants

training grants

research and development grants

rent subsidies

* *Assistance to International Services* financial incentives and other supports towards a range of service businesses which are selling on the export market.

The Industrial Credit Corporation - the state-owned development bank - specialises in the provision of medium and long-term finance for working capital and fixed asset requirements. The Agricultural Credit Corporation (ACC) provides finance for agriculture and businesses based on agricultural products or raw materials.

Approaching the bank for finance

Having thought about your financial requirements and the capital structure of your business, you may very well find yourself having to approach your bank for money. In doing this, there are a number of points you need to keep in mind:

* Open a bank account right at the beginning and establish a relationship with your bank.

* If you lack a financial track record or have no credit rating, you may have difficulties in your dealings with the banks. If married, you may be asked to have your husband sign a guarantee on your behalf. Many women feel strongly about this. Some take their business elsewhere and/or register a strong complaint with the manager, whereas others say that if the banks insist they take a pragmatic position and get their husband's signature.

* Some women in business have found their dealings with banks very frustrating because of unfavourable attitudes towards women entrepreneurs. The best way of fighting such attitudes is to demonstrate how capable you are. Show that you know what you are talking about, that you have done your financial homework and you know the financial implications involved.

* Present yourself as a capable level-headed business woman and you are more likely to be responded to in that fashion.

* Be positive about yourself and your business. There is no need, at this stage, to share any anxieties you may have.

* Be prepared. Successful business women will tell you that knowing what the banks require can make the difference between loan approval and loan refusal.

* If you have very little experience in this area you may find it valuable to enrol in a suitable course available through FAS.

* Familiarise yourself with business terms such as balance sheet, profit and loss statement, assets, liabilities, cash flow projection, security *(see Chapter Six)*.

* To increase your confidence, a very useful exercise is to role-play the bank interview beforehand with your partner or a friend.

* You may already have had grant approval from a state agency but the banks will still require you to go through their procedures. Do not be put off by this. It is what you can expect. So prepare yourself for questions such as the following:

How much money do you need to borrow?

How much money have you to invest yourself?

What will the borrowed money be used for?

In what form is the loan finance required?

What security can you offer to prove you will repay the loan?

Exactly what kind of business are you setting up?

Have you done market research? What size is your market? How competitive are you going to be?

When do you expect the business to begin paying for itself?

How much do you anticipate your business will earn in the first year?

Have you prepared projected profit and loss statements, draft balance sheets and cash flow statements for the period of the proposed loan?

What qualifications and experience do you have that make you think you can succeed?

What expert advice have you had?

Why should your business succeed?

Insurance

Right from the start you need to organise insurance for your business. Particularly in the early stages of business growth, money is likely to be short and it is foolhardy to take needless risks where accidents are concerned where claims could amount to thousands. Machines may break down, your premises may be vandalised, an employee may have an accident - unless you are covered you may find your scarce resources are being used to cover these kinds of event rather than being put into the business. Of course, you cannot insure against all risks. Each kind of insurance costs money so you need to be selective. Get professional advice on the range of policies available, on the costs involved and on the kinds most appropriate for your particular business. When taking out a policy make sure that you read the small print carefully and that you understand your cover fully. These are the main types of insurance policy you will need to think about:

* Fire Insurance
* Burglary
* Cash and valuables
* Malicious damage
* Motor Insurance
* Employer's Liability Insurance

* Public Liability Insurance
* Product Liability
* Life Insurance
* Permanent Health Insurance

Chapter Six

Managing the business

Once you have carried out your initial exploration and planning and your venture is up and going, the key issues then are related to managing the business. The quality of management is central to the success or failure of the venture. You can see why if you consider that it is management that finally controls the use of all the other resources within the business. The key managerial functions are connected with:

* marketing
* finance
* production and operation
* personnel

Do you need training?

You may have acquired skills in one or more of these management areas if you have previously worked in business or in an area related to your chosen venture. Surveys of Irish business women show, however, that many enter business having had little or no management experience. For these women training was a key issue. You too may need to consider joining a training course in some aspect of management. On-the-job learning is very valuable but it is not always necessary to learn by mistakes and you may save yourself money and grief by taking a course. Training need not be a long-term commitment and may simply involve a one-day course or a short series of evening classes. Find out through your local FAS office what state-sponsored training is available. Some VECs and third-level colleges also offer courses which may be useful to you. You may of course have a partner with you in the business who has management skills in the areas where you lack expertise. This is in fact a solution adopted by many successful business women.

Remember your strengths

While it is wise to know your limitations and to attempt to overcome them as far as possible, it is equally important to acknowledge your strengths and abilities. Even if you have not had directly related business experience, through your work in the home, or outside, you will almost certainly have acquired skills and qualities which are important in management. Ability to plan, to think ahead is, for example, a key skill in managing a business and one which you may well have developed either in managing a home and family or at work. Women's up-bringing typically encourages traits of empathy, ability to express positive feelings and a facility in dealing with interpersonal relations. These are characteristics which are currently being recognised as very important in maintaining good employee relations - which is, after all, a key managerial function. The stereotyped image of the manager is the autocratic, confrontational, ruthless and aggressive male. This image is, however, beginning to crumble and nowadays a more co-operative and consultative style of management is promoted as being more effective. Women appear to have a natural affinity for this kind of management - so you are off to a head-start.

Marketing

Successful women entrepreneurs will tell you that marketing plays a central role in their businesses. It is generally agreed that emphasis on marketing is one of the prime ingredients in Japan's major success in today's business world. Marketing in Ireland has, however, been described by one expert in the field as the 'Cinderella of management skills'. If you want to be successful then you need to pay attention to your marketing strategies. Where marketing has become something of a trendy pursuit, it is often associated with a lot of jargon. But do not be put off by this. Marketing, basically, is about letting potential customers know about your product and about keeping your customers satisfied. It is about providing a product or services for which there is a real need; testing out that need; being competitive; getting feedback from the buyer; giving value for money; and providing satisfactory after sales service.

As we said in the previous chapter, you do your market research to establish customer need for your product or service at the very beginning. Once you have identified your target customers, your next step is to let them know that you are providing what they are looking for. You must then, of course, deliver what you promise and at a price that is both profitable for you and good value for the customer. No matter how small your business, right from the start you need to develop a marketing orientation where you keep your view firmly fixed on your customers and their needs. To ensure that you set about marketing in a methodical and planned fashion you should prepare a marketing plan. The headings given below describe the major areas to be included in your plan. Certain areas are more relevant to some types of business than others so tailor the guidelines to meet your own needs.

Have you thought about these?

* projected sales and market share
* product design, packaging and branding
* pricing details
* distribution
* selling methods
* customer profile
* promotion and advertising

To help in drawing up your plan, think about the following questions:

---

* What are your monthly sales targets in terms of size and value for the next two to three years?

* Who are the people who are buying from you? What is their age, education, interests, background occupation? Are they women or men or both? Where are they?

* How are you going to promote your product or service? Do you intend to rely on informal networks and personal contacts? Will you use sales representatives, trade and craft fairs, showrooms, agents, receptions, circulars, free offers?

* Will you use advertisements? How will you advertise - national/ local newspapers, trade press, calendars, posters, leaflets, Golden Pages, local radio, television, cinema? Will you use mail-order or tele-advertising?

---

* What will you charge for each item you sell? In deciding your price, have you taken account of production costs and overheads? Do you know what your competitors charge? Do you intend to compete on the basis of price? Does your price reflect the demand for your product? Have you established a break-even price for your product/service?

* What are your competitive advantages - price, quality, service, reliable deliveries, range of choice?

* How is your product to be packaged? Is the visual appearance likely to be an important factor? Will it have the name or logo of your business on it?

* How will you sell and distribute the goods? Will you use your own or hired transport? Will you use agents? Will you sell from the business? Will you use sales representatives? How many?

Management of finance

If you are like many Irish business women, you will not have had much experience in financial management. Facing up to keeping the books straight can seem like a daunting task if you have no experience in this area. Business women will tell you, however, that it is not as difficult as it might appear. As in other areas, you may need to get training in financial management so check out what is available. Seek out advice, and if you can afford to, use the services of an accountant. Think positively - believe in your ability to deal with financial matters and set out to be efficient. The complexity of record-keeping will, of course, vary according to the sort of business you are running. Whatever your business, however, it is very important to keep up-to-date records and to monitor at all times how your business is faring financially. The heart of your business is the accounting system. The important thing is to start from the beginning with a logical and adequate system. An adequate system basically involves:

* Record-keeping - recording the basic evidence of business transactions such as supplies, invoices, copy sales invoices, bank statements, cheque stubs and so on.
* Book-keeping - recording business transactions in a systematic fashion in a number of books or on a computer.
* Financial statements - annual or other periodical financial accounts.

In drawing up financial statements the key concepts you will need to understand are:

* Profit and Loss Account
* Cash flow Statement
* Balance Sheet

Profit and loss account

Clearly, you cannot continue in business long-term if you are not making a profit. To determine whether or not you are making a profit you need to make an estimate of your sales over a given period, usually each quarter, and then compare this figures with your costs over the same period. In preparing your profit/loss statements you need the following data:

* sales volume
* prime costs (for example, raw materials, packaging, wages, salaries, power)
* gross profit and gross profit percentage of sales
* administration expenses (for example, travel, rent, telephone, advertising, electricity)
* financial charges (for example, bank interest)
* net profit (or loss!)

Sample of summary profit/loss statement

Ms Muffet. For the first year of trading

	Jly	Aug	Sept	etc	Year
			Months		
Sales	6000	9000	8000		152000
Less Cost of Sales					
Materials Used	2400	3600	3200		60800
Production Wages	3000	3000	3000		36000
	5400	6600	6200		96800
Gross Profit (A)	600	2400	1800		55200
Overheads					
Adminisration					
Wages/Salaries	1600	1600	1600		19200
Pension	50	50	50		600
Telephone/Post	100	100	100		1200
Travel	200	200	200		2400
Print/Stationery	150	150	150		1800
Legal/Audit	200	200	200		2400
Sundries	80	80	80		960
	2380	2380	2380		28560
Establishment					
Rent/Rates	600	600	600		7200
Light/Heat	250	250	250		3000
Insurance	100	100	100		1200
Depreciation	200	200	200		2400
Leasing	60	60	60		720
Repairs	50	50	50		600
	1260	1260	1260		15120
Selling					
Advertising	120	120	120		1440
Bad Debts	150	150	150		1800
	270	270	270		3240
Finance					
Bank Interest	50	50	50		600
Bank Charges	40	40	40		480
	90	90	90		1080
Total Overheads (B)	4000	4000	4000		48000
Profit/Loss before tax (A-B)	(3400)	(1600)	(2200)		7200

Cash flow statement

In addition to profitability, you also need to ensure that your business has enough cash to meet its day-to-day requirements. You must ensure that the cash coming into your business each month is sufficient to meet the money you have to pay out. Shortage of cash is one of the commonest causes of business failure so it is very important that you plan for and control your cash flow. A frequent problem reported by women entrepreneurs is that their customers are slow to pay. Women sometimes experience embarrassment in asking for money. Remember that you are only asking for what is due to you and make determined efforts to have money owed paid promptly. You need to decide on a fixed credit policy and on your credit terms. Among your regular customers note those who are reliable, those who need reminding, those you are unsure of, and those to whom you do not wish to give credit at all. Avoid also making large payments in any one time period. It is particularly important to make PAYE payment regularly and *not* to use it for cash flow purposes. Cash flow projections should be drawn up for a period of 18 months at least although most financiers (bank, investors etc) will look for 3 year cash flow projections. To draw up your monthly cash flow statement, you need the following data:

* total receipts (for example, cash purchases, wages and salaries, rent, telephone, heating, travel, loan charges, PAYE, PRSI, VAT).
* net cash money (money is flowing in if total receipts are greater than total payments; there is outflow if payments are greater than receipts).

Balance sheet

Managing and taking control of the finances of your business involves maintaining a balance between profitability and cash flow. Businesses have been known to fail even while they are profitable, because fast growth has depleted cash resources. If you draw up regular statements of profit/loss and cash flow you can spot potential problems and forestall 'hem. Balance sheets are like a snapshot of your business and are designed to indicate that you have the wherewithal to provide your product or service to your target level. To draw up your balance sheet you need the following data:

* total assets including current and fixed assets (for example, cash, prepaid expenses, raw materials, finished goods, work in process, plant and equipment)
* total liabilities including current and long-term (for example, accounts due, taxes, bank payments, wages)
* net worth (total assets minus total liabilities).

Sample of cash flow statement

Ms Muffet Ltd for the first year of trading

	1 Jly	2 Aug	3 Sep	4 Oct	5 Nov	6 Dec	7 Jan	8 Feb	9 Mar	10 Apr	11 May	12 Jun	Year Ended
Receipts													
Sales/Debtors		–	7500	11250	10000	11250	7500	15000	22500	15000	10000	25000	135000
Equity Capital	30000												30000
Bank term loan	8000												8000
Grants													
Total Receipts (A)	38000	–	7500	11250	10000	11250	7500	15000	22500	15000	10000	25000	173000
Payments													
Purchase Materials	–	9250	5750	5250	5750	3000	7250	10250	7250	4000	12500	13250	83500
Production Wages	3000	3000	3000	3000	3000	3000	3000	3000	3000	3000	3000	3000	36000
Wages/Salaries	1600	1600	1600	1600	1600	1600	1600	1600	1600	1600	1600	1600	19200
Pension							600						600
Rent/Rates	1400			1400		800	1400			1400	800		7200
Light/Heat		200			750				750		750		2450
Telephone/Post	20	20	20	260	20	20	260	20	20	260	20	20	960
Insurance	1200												1200
Capital	11500												11500
Leasing	60	60	60	60	60	60	60	60	60	60	60	60	720
Repairs							375						375
Travel		200	200	200	200	200	200	200	200	200	200	200	2200
Print/Stationery	150	150	150	150	150	150	150	150	150	150	150	150	1800
Advertising	450			450			450			450			1800
Legal/Audit					1500			750					2250
Loan Repay		150	150	150	150	150	150	150	150	150	150	150	1650
Bank Int										214			214
Bank Charges				160			160			160			480
VAT		(2760)		2010		1570		3795		2560		5720	12895
Sundries	100	100	100	100	100	100	100	100	100	100	100	100	1200
Total payments (B)	19480	11970	11030	14790	13280	10650	15755	20075	13280	14304	19330	24250	188194
Cash Inflow(A-B)	18520	(11970)	(3530)	(3540)	(3280)	600	(8255)	(5075)	9220	696	(9330)	750	(15194)
Opening Bank Balance	–	18520	6550	3020	(520)	(3800)	(3200)	(11455)	(16530)	(7310)	(6614)	(15944)	–
Closing Bank Balance	18520	6550	3020	(520)	(3800)	(3200)	(11455)	(16530)	(7310)	(6614)	(15944)	(15194)	(15194)

Sample of balance sheet

Ms Muffet at end of the first year

Fixed assets
- costs   9200
- depreciation   2400

- book value   6800

Current assets
Stocks   15000
Debtors   53200

                  68200

Current liabilities
Trade creditors   11250
Sundry creditors & accruals 4806
Bank - overdraft   15194
     - term loan   6550

                  37800

Net current Assets   30400

Net Assets   37200

Shareholders' funds
Share capital   30000
Reserves   7200

                  37200

To provide the information you need in keeping track of your cash flow situation and the profitability of your business you must keep up-to-date accounts. The Revenue Commissioners will also need to see these and your VAT and PAYE records. The banks and state agencies will also be interested in them if you have sought funding from them. Your method of record-keeping will need to be tailored to the individual needs of your business. Basic requirements include:

* Receipts and payments record - this is a record of all monies (cash or cheques) being received and paid out by the company.

* Sales ledger - this records business with customers which is done on credit. One side of the sales ledger records each credit sale, the date when it is invoiced and value of the goods sent out. On the opposite side payments received are recorded. At the end of the month invoices and receipts are totalled separately, the difference between the two reflecting the customer's debt or otherwise.

* Purchases ledger - this records transactions with suppliers from whom you buy goods or services on credit. One side of the ledger lists all purchase invoices giving date, number and amount. The opposite side lists payments towards these purchases. At the end of the month, subtracting total payments from total purchases indicates how much the supplier is owed.

* Petty Cash record - this records cash payments for small day- to-day debts or other expenses that have to be settled immediately.

* Wages record - this records each employee's name, personal details, date of joining the business, promotions, current position, basic wage, overtime payments, sick leave record and so on.

Most stationery shops sell a range of pre-printed account records. Unless you are starting a business on a very small scale, all aspects of financial management will be greatly simplified and speeded up if you have a computer. It is well worth raising some additional finance, if necessary, to buy the appropriate hardware (computer) and software (programmes). A good accounts package is likely to become the base and backbone of your business. It will enable you to keep accurate records, make rational projections and also reduce your audit fees. You should seek professional advice and also talk to someone in business already using the system you are interested in, before you purchase either hardware or software.

Value-Added Tax (VAT)

Unless your business is very small, you will almost certainly have to register for Value-Added Tax (VAT). Regulations vary but up-to-date information can be obtained from the Revenue Commissioners. Even if your annual turnover is below the threshold for which you are legally obliged to register, it may in some cases be to your advantage to register anyhow and you should check this out. Registration and accounting for VAT can be a complicated subject so it is advisable to seek professional advice on what needs to be done. The Revenue Commissioners have issued a booklet, *Guide To The Value-added Tax*, which you may find useful. The registration form for VAT can be had from your local tax office. On receipt of your completed form you will be issued a particular VAT registration number.

Pay As You Earn (PAYE) and
Pay Related Social Insurance (PRSI)

Anyone you pay regularly must be registered as an employee and must have a TFA in respect of your employment. Returns are made monthly of PAYE/PRSI and an annual return, ie P 35, must also be made.

Management of operations

If your business venture is small, then management of operations should not present too many difficulties. Whether you are in a manufacturing, service or retail business there are certain common issues that you will need to deal with. It is, for example, important that you keep yourself informed. 'Keeping an ear to the ground' can be a help but seeking out information in a systematic fashion is likely to be more useful. Ask yourself:

*   Is your market information up-to-date?
*   Are you keeping track of your competitors?
*   What developments or technological advances are happening in your area?
*   Are you in touch with aspects of the economic climate that might affect your business?

In providing your product or service, other aspects of management you must deal with include:

* location
* facilities
* equipment
* labour force
* suppliers

Ask yourself:

* What are the major advantages and disadvantages of your location? For example, closeness to customers or suppliers, access to transport, availability of labour.
* Do you have the facilities you require? for example, land space, office space, storage or warehousing space.
* Do you have up-to-date equipment? Is it running efficiently? Are there any problems with your equipment?
* Have you as many workers as you need? Do they have the required skills? Is training needed? Is it easy to recruit appropriately skilled workers? How do you keep labour turnover down? How do you keep the rate of absenteeism low?
* Can you find the suppliers you need? Have you more than one source of supply in case of emergency? Are supplies delivered on time? Do suppliers give value for money?

If you are in a manufacturing business then there are other areas of production management with which you or your partners will have to deal. You will need to know about:

* the production process itself and the constraints which operate on time, cost and quality
* inventory control - keeping track of goods in process and finished goods
* quality control - setting up inspection systems and standards for control of quality of raw materials, goods in process and finished goods
* production scheduling and flow - managing work schedules, planning production flow, setting new schedules for increasing production
* production monitoring - noting time of acceptance of orders and dates of completion

*   stock control - keeping track of quantity of goods in stock, withdrawal of stock, minimum stock level.

Personnel management

If you are employing others in your business then a key aspect of management will be setting up and maintaining good employer- employee relations. Women seem to have a particular facility in dealing with employer-employee relations and many women entrepreneurs say that this is their prime managerial strength. Your main tasks here are to create an atmosphere in the workplace that motivates your employees to give of their best, to press for good work and to reward for work well done. If you are in a local employment initiative or in a co-operative, then you may have some different issues to deal with in establishing good working relationships with the others involved. A key factor here will be your ability to work well as a team member with others in pursuing common goals. Of prime importance will be your openness to differences of opinion, willingness to listen, discuss and talk out difficulties. The following pointers will help you to ensure good labour relations. Check through these and think about your own level of skill in each area.

Pointers for good employer-employee relations	My level of skill
Set a good example yourself. Do not ask of others what you yourself are not willing to do	
Do not set too high a standard and do not expect too much of others	
Accentuate the positive. Give praise for work well done	
Encourage employees to take responsibility	
Delegate responsibility	
Provide clear instructions on duties and responsibilities	
Give guidance and assistance when these are needed	
Be fair and do not blame others for your own mistakes or limitations	
Deal with mistakes in a direct, straightforward, non-blaming manner	
Give regular feedback on performance	

Pointers for good employer-employee relations	My level of skill
Value your employees as people, not just for their performance	
Acknowledge that employees have needs and lives outside of work	
Confront problems or difficulties openly and stay with them until they are resolved	
Encourage employees to develop their skills and capabilities	
Take negative feedback without becoming defensive or argumentative	
Be willing to actively manage, supervise and control the activities of others	
Set up clear lines of communication to and from management and employees	
Establish clear areas of responsibility and structures for accountability	
Be approachable and courteous	
Allow some degree of employee participation in decision-making	

Apart from maintaining good labour relations, if you have others working for you in your business, there are some administrative and practical issues with which you will also have to deal:

* *PAYE and PRSI:* You will need to register for PAYE and PRSI. Income tax (PAYE) and pay related social insurance (PRSI) will have to be deducted from employees' wages and paid over to the Revenue Commissioners. Details are available in the 'Employer's Guide to PAYE and PRSI' issued by the Revenue Commissioners.

* *Employment Legislation:* there are certain legal obligations on you as an employer of which you need to be aware. There is legislation, for example, on terms and conditions of employment, safety in industry, dismissal procedures, maximum notice, redundancy, employment equality and discrimination, maternity leave and holidays.

* *Employer's Liability Insurance:* You will need to take out insurance to protect your employees against any accident occurring on your business premises for which you could be responsible.
* *Pensions:* As your business develops you will need to consider introducing a company pension scheme. You should seek professional advice on this matter.

Chapter Seven

Growing concerns: Business issues

As we have discussed, businesses grow and develop through different stages from the decision to start-up through consolidation to take-off and expansion. Success does not necessarily mean that your business should get to the stage of growth and expansion. Success is defined in terms of your goals and aims for your business and you may not be interested in growth. For you, the fact that the venture has started up and is surviving may be sufficient success. Or your primary goal may be to stay small and focus on consolidation. You may also, however, have your sights set on growth. Not all business people are alike and different types have different approaches to the growth and development of their businesses. Consider the descriptions given below of these different types of business person and decide for yourself what future direction you want for your business.

Orientation to growth?	*Is this what I want?*
Life-Style Entrepreneur Your primary objective is to have a life-style that enables you to be creative and autonomous. You have no interest in growth.	
Survival Entrepreneur Your main objective is to be successfully self-employed, with no ambition for expansion.	
Limited Growth Entrepreneur You are interested in growth within set limits. Control of the business both in terms of ownership and the quality of what you produce is important.	
Growth entrepreneur You are alert and responsive to all opportunities for the successful growth of your business.	

The problems faced and the skills necessary in managing a large business are different to those involved in running a small concern. Not everyone is suited to big business and you need to think carefully about the kind of business that best suits you.

Your orientation to growth may, of course, change over time. Studies show that an important influence can be the existing stage in the life-cycle of the woman entrepreneur and that of her family, if she has children. Some business women say that their attitude to growth changed as family responsibilities, especially in relation to childcare, became less as they moved through different stages of their lives.

Exporting

There are different routes to expansion. You may extend the range of goods on offer so that, for example, if you are producing beachwear you branch out into party-wear. Another means of expansion is to start making some component of your product which, up to now, you have been buying in. A further avenue for expansion is, of course, to start exporting. Export is particularly significant in the context of 1992 and the Single European Act which will make the European Community into a large area without internal frontiers allowing free movement of goods, services and capital. Exporting has the advantage of opening up larger markets for your products. It also makes you less vulnerable should there be a fall-off in the home-market and it can be very profitable. Because exporting is important to the health of the national economy, if you have realistic export possibilities, you will be given state support and assistance. A comprehensive booklet giving detailed information on the whole area is available from the Irish Export Board (Coras Trachtála - CTT).

Exporting can, however, be a complicated and risky business. You need to be familiar with the necessary documentation and various regulations. You may have to deal with any problems that arise in a foreign language. It may be more difficult to find customers abroad or the product may have to be adapted to suit foreign needs. You will also need to take into account that the cost of your product will increase because of extra costs such as transport or commission to an agent or distributor. Any problems you experience at home - for example, getting money from a customer - are likely to be magnified when you are operating from a distance. Because of these kinds of factors you need to be sure that exporting is worth it, Ask yourself if you have really exploited the home-market or could you just as easily sell at home?

If you have decided to export you need to plan very carefully and carry out research. Adopting an attitude of 'try it and see how it works out' is unlikely to be successful. Get all the help and advice you can. Contact CTT and other state agencies who can give you valuable help in identifying the best opportunities for your product. Use the extensive library resources of CTT to find out market information in the countries you are interested in exploring. If possible, visit trade fairs where you will have an opportunity to study the competition, compare prices and meet potential customers. CTT can advise you also on displaying your product at leading foreign trade fairs where Irish stands are often organised.

One of the decisions you will have to make is how you are going to service your market abroad. Most exporters sell either through an agent or a distributor. An agent will seek out orders for you, for which s/he gets paid a commission. An agent will not arrange supply and is not responsible for collecting payment. A distributor buys stock from you and resells it to customers and collecting payments is his/her own responsibility. CTT can advise you on how to contact agents and distributors. Choosing an agent or distributor is an important decision so you need to check out carefully beforehand the reputation of the person you hire.

You will also have to think about pricing for foreign markets. In quoting a price you must be very clear on what it includes - does it include, for example, shipping costs and insurance? It is important in discussing prices that you and your customer are talking about the same thing. Export prices are usually followed by one of the following sets of initials:

CIF (Cost, Insurance, Freight) a price with this set of initials means that the cost of goods along with insurance and freight charges for delivering the goods to the final destination are covered.

FOB (Free On Board) this means a price including the cost of delivering the goods on board ship but not the cost of freight or insurance to the destination port.

You must also be aware of the documentation required in exporting your goods:

* an export specification form, usually in triplicate, is required for all goods exported from Ireland. One copy goes to the customs office at point of exit, one goes to the Central Statistics Office and the third may be returned to you, on request, as your own record.

* an export licence is required for some goods including agricultural items.

* an exchange control declaration form is required when the value of the consignment is over a certain limit. Check with CTT for the up-to-date limit.

* a commercial invoice must accompany all goods exported. The invoice must be signed by the exporter and give: names and addresses of exporter and buyer, a description of the goods exported, weight, amount, price per unit and total price of consignment, statements of terms of sale, discounts - if any - and shipping arrangements.

* goods from one EC country to another must be accompanied by a transit form.

* a consignment note or airway bill is a receipt from a shipping company or airline confirming that the goods specified have been received for transport to the stated destination.

* a bill of landing is a receipt for goods delivered on board and also legal evidence that a contract has been made to deliver them to the stated destination. This document must be sent to the buyer abroad to enable her/him take possession of the goods.

Because of the considerable work and effort involved, it is important at the outset that you think through carefully your answers to the following questions:

* Can you get the necessary working capital to develop export sales?
* Can your business afford the extra cash investment needed?
* Has your product a significant advantage over the likely foreign competition?
* Is the foreign market buoyant enough to make the extra work and cost worthwhile?
* Can you sell your product at a competitive price in spite of extra costs involved?
* How are you going to find potential customers?
* Are the sales strategies you use at home likely to be suitable in the foreign market?
* Has your business got the necessary management skills for export trade?
* Are your home sales likely to suffer if you or your employees have to spend time abroad?
* Does your business have the production capacity to serve the export market without disrupting your home market?

Planning for growth

Whatever avenue you choose for the growth and expansion of your business, it is a process that needs to be carefully planned.

A common cause of failure among basically profitable firms is attempting expansion too soon and too quickly. In developing sound strategies for growth you need to consider the following key issues:

Key issues related to yourself

What are your goals for the business?

What are your goals for yourself?

What level of expertise do you (or members of your team) have in relation to important functions such as financial management, marketing, producing, managing distribution?

How high would you rate your ability to manage the activities of others?

How willing are you to delegate responsibility?

How good are you at planning ahead?

How well do your strengths, and weaknesses match the goals you have set for your business?

Do you know the pressures and demands that will be involved?

Are you prepared to give the commitment that is required?

Key issues related to your business

Finance Do you have capital/assets or is borrowing required?

Personnel Do you have the staff you require in terms of numbers, skills, quality of work?

Production Do you have the production resources needed in terms of, for example, manufacturing processes, technology, distribution processes, suppliers, quality control?

Marketing Do you have the required marketing resources in terms of, for example, market share, customer relations, information systems?

Management Resources Do you have the required management expertise to control an expanded business effectively?

The experience of successful growth-orientated Irish women entrepreneurs provide certain pointers to good practice in formulating strategy for the expansion of one's business. These guidelines are given below.

Guidelines for good practice

* Analyse your motives.
* Try to stand back from your business and be as objective as possible in evaluating its strengths and weaknesses.
* Identify expected benefits and drawbacks of expansion and take account of these in developing strategy.
* Identify and think about different options for growth - developing export trade, diversification, expansion of range, alternative markets, technology transfer.
* Seek out information and sources of advice.
* Evaluate thoroughly, centering on financial viability and performance, marketing capacity, operation and production resources, management capabilities.
* Reassess your growth plan in the light of the outcomes of your analysis.

If you are intent on growth and expansion and if your business is in manufacturing, remember that the IDA and Shannon Development Company have a particular Company Development Programme which focuses on growth-oriented business. This programme is designed to develop the required management expertise as well as providing cash incentives. Check out this programme with your regional office of the IDA, Shannon Development and Udarás na Gaeltachta.

Chapter Eight

Growing concerns: Personal issues

Managing your personal life, looking after yourself, is a key element in being a successful business woman. When you are calm and relaxed, fit and healthy and have a positive outlook you have the energy to handle difficult decisions, face problems, see creative solutions and do the tasks that need to be done. Looking after yourself may be particularly pertinent for you as a woman since research shows that women entering the world of business sometimes experience higher levels of stress than men. This is so because of factors such as lack of role models, lack of experience, role conflict and feelings of guilt. It is well known that while a certain level of stress can be motivating and energising, overly high levels of stress lead to all sorts of physical, personal, interpersonal and work-related problems. It is important, then, both for your own sake and the sake of your business, that you put looking after yourself high up on the list of your priorities.

Running a business, particularly in the early stages of venture formation, may take up a large amount of your time and energy. It is important, however, to aim for balance in your life so that aspects other than work are not neglected. Our lives are multifaceted and we need to pay attention to all aspects - intellectual, emotional, social, physical, sensual, spiritual and creative.

Thought influences action

Perhaps you have come across the saying 'energy follows thought'. The idea is that if you put your focus on positive events, on successful outcomes and happenings and on satisfying interactions, you will attract these in your life. If, on the other hand, your outlook on life is mainly negative then your experiences will likewise be negative. Whether or not you can influence external events, such as winning the lottery, through positive thinking is something you will have to experiment with in your own life!

However, psychologists have shown that there is no doubt that the way we think, the kind of mental messages we give ourselves, have a very great influence on how we feel about things and, consequently, on how we behave. For example, if you entertain such negative thoughts as 'I'd never be able to make a go of a business', then the chances are that you will begin to act in certain ways that very definitely decrease your chances of being a successful entrepreneur. If, however, you have a positive image of yourself as a woman who has got what it takes, then the likelihood is that you will have the energy to create the circumstances and carry out the actions that fulfil this image. Concentrating on negative aspects of life can make you feel hopeless and helpless whereas focusing on the positive side of things gives you the energy and motivation to act constructively.

Having a positive outlook not only increases your own sense of well-being but affects others around you and helps them also to take action and move forward in their lives. While the benefits of positive thinking may seem very obvious, many people are more inclined to give themselves negative rather than positive messages.

The first step in changing your outlook is to start becoming aware of the particular negative messages which you give yourself. Being aware of your negative self-statements, your next step is to put a stop to them and to substitute more positive messages. Below are some common forms of negative thinking. Check through these, see if any of them are habitual to you and, if so, see what positive statements you can give yourself instead. For example, if you are in the habit of saying to yourself 'I'd never be able to cope with record keeping', try substituting something like 'I haven't had much experience with record keeping, but I am an intelligent woman and I can learn'.

Forms of negative thinking	*Your positive alternative*
Catastrophising For example, you make a mistake and you tell yourself that 'this is just awful, or a catastrophe, or a disaster'.	
Over-generalisation For example, on a few occasions you fail to deal directly with a badly-done job and you tell yourself 'I'm *always* doing that'.	

Forms of negative thinking	Your positive alternative
Screening Out Positive Feedback For example, several colleagues react favourably to a presentation you have made but one person reacts critically. It is this negative reaction that you remember and brood on and you say to yourself 'this is the feedback that really counts'.	
Setting Rigid Requirements For example, if your performance is less than perfect, you say to yourself 'I'm a total failure'.	
'Gloom and Doom' Thinking For example, your initial choice of a business partner fails to work out and you tell yourself ' what's the point, I'll never find the person I want'.	
Putting Negative Labels On Yourself For example, you fail to foresee some difficulty and you tell yourself 'what a fool, I'm a right idiot'.	
'If Only' Thinking For example, your customer numbers are down and you say to yourself 'if only the customers weren't so picky and choosy' instead of looking at the feedback and seeing how it can be used.	
'Should' and 'Have To' Thinking For example, you tell yourself 'I should do the housework after work in the evening' instead of realising you *could* do this and you have a choice.	
Making Assumptions For example, you see your employees talking and laughing at teabreak and you say to yourself 'I bet they are laughing at the stupid mistake I made this morning'.	

Owning responsibility for your life

Successful entrepreneurs take the view that how things turn out in their lives is very much their own responsibility and is less dependent on luck or chance or fate than on their own initiative and actions. Adopting this kind of active stance is often difficult for women as we have been brought up to see ourselves more as passive bystanders rather than as persons who influence and are responsible for what happens in our lives. If we are to move forward, to make changes, to take charge, we need to own our responsibility for how things are - own our responsibility for:

* our thoughts
* our feelings
* our actions
* our needs
* our problems
* our achievements

You may think that taking responsibility for your life in this way puts an enormous burden on you. The opposite, however, is true - owning responsibility liberates you and gives you power. You realise that nobody makes you think, feel or act in any particular way - how you are is how you choose to be. For example, if you feel angry and you frame the situation as 'you make me angry', then you are in the power of the other person. If, however, you own the anger and say 'I am angry' then the implication is that the feeling is yours, and the power is yours to see the situation in other ways if you want. You are adopting an active rather than a passive stance. Similarly, if you are experiencing a problem with, for example, your workforce, you can frame the problem as follows: 'if only my employees weren't such an inefficient and apathetic lot, my business would operate fine.' Laying the problem at the feet of your employees puts it outside your control. If, on the other hand, you own the problem as yours and frame it in terms of how you can best motivate and train your workers, then you can start to do something about it. Likewise, if you own responsibility for your achievements and successes, then they belong to you and you can use them to build your self-worth and increase your risk-taking ability.

When you own responsibility for your needs you can begin to take active steps to have them addressed rather than waiting for someone to notice what you want. For example, if you need help with the housework, rather than going around in a huff waiting for your partner to divine your need, you can ask directly for certain tasks to be done.

The importance of feelings

Generally, feelings get very bad publicity. They are regarded as irrational, silly, childish, dangerous or suspect. We are brought up to keep a tight rein on our feelings. We are told, for example, 'to keep cool', 'be brave', 'don't let them see you're nervous', 'don't cry', 'there's nothing to be frightened of'. Our educational system emphasises intellectual development with little attention to emotional development. Feelings, however, are what give richness, colour and depth to our lives. Moreover, feelings are a very important source of information for us. When you experience an uncomfortable feeling, such as anger, this is a signal to you that something is going wrong in the interaction or situation and that you need to take some action. Positive feelings, on the other hand, indicate that the interaction or situation is satisfactory or non-threatening to you. Suppressing or denying your feelings means that you are ignoring important information and is one of the prime factors in interpersonal difficulties. Far from being airy-fairy, feelings are real physical events - what you experience as a feeling is the result of complex changes going on in your body. If you bear this in mind, then you may be less inclined to ignore or dismiss them.

Women are so often accused of being over-emotional or irrational at work, that they often fall over backwards to avoid showing any feelings at all. It is inevitable, however, that feelings such as anger, frustration, annoyance, worry, regret, delight or pleasure, will arise and it is important to be able to deal with them. The first step is to acknowledge and accept your feeling - whatever it is. This may sometimes be sufficient in itself: for example, while at an important meeting you become annoyed by a needless interruption, you register your annoyance but decide not to do anything more than take a few deep breaths. There will be times, however, when it is appropriate and very important that you do take a second step and verbally express your feeling. In expressing your feeling it is important that you send an 'I message' - for example, 'I feel angry' - rather than a 'you message' such as 'you are such a bully you make me feel so mad'. Sending a 'you message' which labels or attacks or puts down the other person will almost always result in aggression or defensiveness. Using an 'I message' which lets the other person know your feeling in a straightforward, honest manner increases the chances of keeping communication open between you. It takes practice, however, to stick with 'I messages' and not to resort to blaming or labelling. Your expression of your feeling will carry more weight where your body language is conveying the same message as your words. For example, the other person is more likely to take account of your expression of anger if you can look her/him straight in the eye, if your voice is firm and you do not have a nervous smile playing on your face.

Tackling stress

Stress may be defined as your body's responses - both physical and mental - to the demands of your life-style. When you think of the word 'stress' you probably think of negative experiences such as feeling exhausted, irritable, tense, or overwrought. Stress, however, is not always bad for you. We are constantly under some amount of stress and at reasonable levels it motivates us, increases our alertness and pushes us to action. A certain level of stress, for example, can put you on your mettle and help you prepare for an important meeting. Some people feel they always work better under pressure and really enjoy the challenge of a tight schedule or deadline. Problems only arise when we have too much stress or experience it for too long. When stress becomes too much or long-term, we may become permanently worked-up and in a constant state of tension which causes us to fall ill and to function badly. The ill-effects of long-term stress may show up in different aspects of our lives:

Behavioural   For example, excessive alcohol consumption, cigarette smoking, over-eating, drug abuse, restlessness

Physiological   For example, high blood pressure, increased heart rate, muscle tension

Emotional For example, decreased concentration, forgetfulness, heightened sensitivity to criticism.

Work-related   For example, job dissatisfaction, poor productivity, absenteeism.

The same stress that can motivate and energise you can also make you ill, or even kill you, unless you take steps to keep it to a manageable level. Different people can tolerate different levels of stress so you need to decide for yourself what a tolerable level is for you.

The first step in reducing your stress level is to become aware of what personally causes you stress. The sources of stress are many and include the following:

* **changes** in our lives such as getting a new job
* **work stressors** such as difficulties in commuting, low job satisfaction, technological change
* **environmental stressors** such as noise, extreme heat or cold, pollution, cigarette smoke
* **emotional stressors** such as jealousy, fear, worry, bereavement
* **social stressors** such as isolation, loneliness, crime

* **economic and political stressors** such as unemployment, cost of housing, high taxes
* **physical stressors** such as pain, illness, disease, pregnancy
* **family stressors** such as unequal sharing of workload, role conflict, money difficulties, differences in lifestyle, caring for an aged parent.

Make a list of the main causes of stress in your life. Think about the different types of stressors listed above and see if you need to include something from each of them. Tick those items which are the greatest source of stress and think about what you can do to change the situation.

A second step in tackling stress is to recognise the particular symptoms which serve as warning signals that you are over- stressed. these symptoms may be:

Physical such as skin rash, headache, asthma, diarrhoea, back pain, stomach problems.

Mental such as forgetfulness, poor judgement, tendency to fly off-the-handle, more frequent mistakes, being lost for words.

Behavioural such as overeating, smoking, insomnia, 'butter fingers', over-reacting, not listening, talking too fast.

Emotional such as tearfulness, short tempered, withdrawn, snappy, low confidence, apathetic.

Draw up a list of your personal warning signals and mark those which you experience most frequently.

Knowing what causes you stress and recognising your particular warning signals, you can then begin to do something constructive to tackle the problem. Just as stress may manifest itself in physical, mental, behavioural and emotional symptoms so too an effective stress management programme will incorporate these different aspects of life. Use the following checklist to help you devise your own programme. We have already dealt with many of the items on the checklist but in some cases you may need to do some further reading and explore the area more fully. Some useful references are provided at the end of the book.

Check-list for stress management

Physical
* healthy diet
* regular exercise
* relaxation
* taking rest periods during the day
* treating yourself

Mental
* developing a positive outlook
* focusing on solutions rather than on problems
* developing the habit of positive self-talk
* affirming yourself for your strengths, good qualities, achievements and successes
* letting go of the past

Emotional
* valuing your feelings
* using your feelings for the information they give
* expressing your feelings appropriately (especially anger)
* physical release of tension

Behavioural
* setting goals and establishing priorities
* planning and organisation of work and home life
* time management
* problem solving
* assertiveness (including making requests, setting limits, handling criticism, standing up for your rights, dealing with confrontation)

Social
* having a supportive social network
* having friend(s) you can depend on
* having satisfying leisure pursuits
* engaging in social outings

Family and Home
* having a supportive partner and family
* working out satisfactory homecare arrangements
* compatible life-styles
* sharing of values and interests

Managing home and work and life-style

When you talk to women who have set up in business, one of the key concerns that they will tell you they have is their management of home life and work. We know from their experience that the position of women in business cannot meaningfully be discussed without reference to their domestic responsibilities. Unlike the experience of men, for whom work and home are almost always clearly separated, women in business are frequently trying to reconcile a dual commitment to family and to business. It is important to think about these issues at all stages of setting up and running a business. Here are a number of issues for you to think about - see how they apply to you and then make a determined effort to address them.

What is the level of support, both practical and psychological, from your spouse/partner in running:

* your home
* your business
* your relationship
* your family

Level of support from spouse/ partner	Things we Need to Change	Action Plan
Home		
Business		
Relationship		
Family		

Questions to Ask Yourself	Things to Work Through	Action Plan

* Do you feel guilty about taking time for yourself?
* Do you feel guilty when you are working in your business and feel you should be at home?
* Do you feel guilty when you are at home working and feel that you should be concentrating on your business?
* What are the main constraints that running a business imposes on your personal life?
* What are the main constraints that running a business imposes on your leisure life?
* What are the main constraints that running a business imposes on your family life?
* Do you organise:
  - your home life?
  - personal relationships?
  - leisure time?
  - social life?
* Do you plan your priorities in relation to:
  - home life?
  - personal relationships?
  - leisure time?
  - social life?
* Do you have clear objectives in relation to:
  - home life?
  - personal relationships?
  - leisure time?
  - social life?		

Successful business women can and do manage to reconcile their home lives and their business. However, they will tell you that they have had to work hard to overcome the guilt they felt. It is possible for you to be an entrepreneurial manager in relation to your personal life, family and life-style, as well as in your business. But do not take this for granted. You will need to consciously work at it. Surround yourself with people who give you positive support, who emphasise the fact that you have both the capacity and the right to take control of all areas of your life. Beware of the danger of trying to prove yourself to others on all fronts. It is your life. Coming to terms with yourself and all facets of your life is being truly enterprising. Setting up in business gives you the autonomy, confidence and self-fulfilment to look at your life and the choices you have.

Chapter Nine

Being an enterprising person

Being in business - from the decision to start-up, to getting underway and managing the venture - requires a combination of skills. You need, for example, to know the mechanics of producing your goods or running your service - these are your operational skills. Further skills are required to keep the show on the road - these are your managerial skills. Previous chapters have discussed some of these operational and managerial skills. This chapter deals with another set of skills equally important in running a business - these are your entrepreneurial skills. Being an enterprising person is not just about having bright ideas; it also involves skills in, for example, seeking solutions, in organising and planning and in goal-setting. These are skills which, of course, are not just important in business but in all areas of life. You can also be an enterprising person in your home and personal life.

Communicating effectively

In being an enterprising person, one skill which is very important is your ability to communicate clearly and directly. Poor communication gives rise to all sorts of problems and misunderstandings and creates much frustration and confusion. Clear communication, like any other skill, has to be learned and practised. Some guidelines to effective communication are presented overleaf. Check through these and think about your own level of skill in this area.

Guidelines for effective communication	My level of skill?
Remember that the same word may have different meanings for different people. Check that the other person is receiving the message you intended to send.	
Avoid incomplete or hurried messages where the other person is left trying to guess what you wanted to say.	
Avoid double messages where you are saying one thing and meaning another.	
Remember that, apart from the words you use, your body language is also conveying a message. Your message will be confusing if you are saying one thing verbally and something else with your body language.	
In expressing your needs, feelings or problems, try to be honest and straightforward and send 'I messages' which imply your own responsibility in the matter, rather than 'you messages'.	
Give your attention to the message you want to give. If you are preoccupied or distracted you are likely to send a confusing message.	
Look at the person you are talking to and get her/his attention before you speak.	
Attempting to ignore strong emotions, such as anger, may cause you to become inarticulate. Pay attention to your feeling and try to find a way of expressing it appropriately.	
Try to minimise interruptions or interferences such as noise or uncomfortable temperature.	
Listen attentively to what the other person is saying.	
Pay attention and show understanding of the other person's feelings.	

Handling confrontation

Whether in running your business or in your personal life, there will be occasions when you need to confront someone on some problem between you. It can often be very difficult for women to give this kind of critical feedback. However, following the dictum 'if you don't have anything nice to say, don't say anything at all' can cause many misunderstandings and create tension and frustration. It is important to be able to give feedback in a way that opens up the problem and, at the same time, leaves the other person's self-esteem and self-respect as undiminished as possible. Guidelines on handling confrontation are given below. Check through these and think about your own level of skill in each area outlined.

Guidelines for Handling Confrontation	My level of Skill?
Deal with the problem when it first arises rather than allowing the difficulty build up.	
Choose the place and time for confrontation wisely. It is inappropriate, for example, to raise a difficulty with someone in front of their workmates or just as s/he is about to get the bus home.	
Tackle the problem not the person	
Be specific. Describe the behaviour and how it affects you, rather than putting a label on the person.	
Spell out what you need the person to do to resolve the problem.	
Watch out for cues that the person is willing to deal with the problem and acknowledge her/his efforts.	
Allow the other person give their side of things.	
Allow for the possibility of compromise.	
Agree how to avoid recurrence of the problem.	
Don't use the situation to bring up lots of old issues - deal with one thing at time.	
Don't confront on the basis of hearsay.	
If possible, end on a positive note.	

Effective problem-solving

The manner in which you approach a problem greatly influences your ability to resolve it satisfactorily. A haphazard or scattered approach will make any problem seem difficult. On the other hand, adopting a systematic step-by-step approach can enable you tackle even problems that at first appearance seem to be insurmountable. Research shows that the stepsdescribed below comprise the basic ingredients of effective problem solving.

Steps in problem-solving

* Define what the problem is. People involved in the problem should be included in defining the issue. aim to be specific. Ask questions: what? when? where? how? who?

* Think of all the different possible solutions to the problem. Try to be as creative as possible in seeking solutions. It may be helpful to use the technique of brainstorming.

* Evaluate the pros and cons of the different solutions. Assess consequences.

* Choose one solution and commit yourself to it. Draw up a plan of action. Decide who is to carry out the plan and what resources are needed.

* Carry out your plan of action.

* Monitor the outcomes and side-effects of your plan of action.

* Review the success of your problem-solving efforts. If the problem still exists you may need to return to your initial step.

Time management

An important element in tackling stress and in ensuring a harmonious balance between your work, personal life and leisure is your ability to manage time. If you do not learn to organise your life, you are in danger of ending up with 'hurry sickness' where everything you do is subject to panic pressures and time shortage. Check through the following danger signals of 'hurry sickness' and see if any of them apply to you:

* feeling constantly tired and worn-out
* working long hours every day of the week
* bringing work home every evening
* not having enough time for home or social life
* always rushing
* doing several things at the one time
* habitually working at crisis pitch
* frequently missing deadlines
* always trying to catch up on jobs
* not having time to take a break and eat a proper lunch
* bringing work away on holidays

The key to effective time management is systematic planning based on the important goals in your life. The next section deals more fully with systematic goal-setting and with identifying your top- priority goals. The guidelines given below provide further pointers to time management:

* Keep your sights set on what you want to achieve in life. Set goals for yourself.
* Decide which are your top priority goals.
* Schedule your time according to your priorities
* Ensure you include time for a satisfying personal and family life in your schedule.
* Ensure you include time for leisure and relaxation in your schedule.
* Draw up a list of the tasks and activities required to meet your priority goals.
* Draw up a time-table for carrying out the necessary tasks and activities - what has to be done within a year, a month, a week, tomorrow.
* Make a list of things you have to do each day. Put them in order of importance and work through them from the most to the least important.
* Keep a diary where daily meetings and appointments are noted.
* Set limits to your accessibility. For example, set times when you are not to be interrupted by phone-calls or visitors.
* Learn to say 'no' when you need to say no.
* Avoid doing tasks that can appropriately be delegated to others.
* Do one thing at a time.
* Set up an efficient filing system.
* Keep your work-space tidy.
* Keep items constantly needed easy-to-hand.

Setting goals

This chapter ends with goal-setting which is a key skill not only in successful entrepreneurship but in all areas of life. Setting goals and establishing priorities gives you a sense of purpose and direction in life, it increases your motivation and helps you to anticipate difficulties and to work more efficiently. Goal-setting also builds your sense of self-worth - as you reach one goal, this reinforces your self-confidence and strengthens your motivation to achieve other goals. In this way, you get a sense of progressing in your life and this enhances your self-worth. To be of any value to you, the goals you set must be:

* realistic
* specific
* measurable
* time phased (specify what will be accomplished over a certain period of time)

The steps given below are the basic ingredients of goal-setting. Use these steps to help you in planning your goals in life.

Steps in goal-setting

* Write down all the things you want to achieve in the next five years. Think about your business, your home life, your personal relationships, your social life, your emotional life, your health.

* From your list of goals, select those which you want to achieve in the next year.

* Pick your top three most important goals.

    First priority goal

    Second priority goal

    Third priority goal

* Review your three high-priority goals and refine and clarify them so that they are realistic, specific and measurable. Re-write your three goals.

    First priority goal

    Second priority goal

    Third priority goal

---

* Take each of your three top-priority goals and think about the particular action steps you need to take to reach that goal. Work out a time-table: what has to be done within a month, a week, tomorrow?

  Action Steps To First Priority

  Action Steps To Second Priority

  Action Steps To Third Priority

* Think about the obstacles that might prevent you from reaching your goal.

  Obstacles To First Priority

  Obstacles To Second Priority

  Obstacles To Third Priority

* Think about the help and resources you can draw on to reach your goals.

  Help and Resources For First Priority

  Help and Resources For Second Priority

  Help and Resources For Third Priority

You need self-discipline and time to systematically plan your goals in life in the manner described above. More importantly, however, you need to be committed to your goals. Goal-setting is a pointless exercise unless you are resolved to take the steps necessary to make your goals a reality.

Remember that your plan is not immutable. It is meant to be an aid in taking charge of your life and is not meant to restrict or confine you. Accordingly, it is important to periodically review and revise your goals.

Action

You have now considered some of the key issues which arise at different stages of business formation - from the decision to start-up, to managing a growing business. You have reviewed your commitment and motivation and considered the pressures and demands that will be made on you. You have reviewed your expertise in different areas of management and have thought about building a business team. You have assessed your needs for information and advice and have thought about how these might be met. You have considered the rewards and satisfactions involved.

Now you are ready for action!

Use your skills in problem-solving and goal-setting to plan where you go from here. Ensure that you build-in looking after yourself in your plan. Finally, remember what women who have started up in business say - **'if you have a good idea, just go ahead and do it'**.

Useful Addresses

ACC (Agricultural Credit Corporation Ltd), ACC House, Upper Hatch St, Dublin 2 (01) 780644

An Bord Pleanála, Irish Life Centre, Lower Abbey St, Dublin 1 (01) 728011

Bord Fáilte (Bord Fáilte Eireann - The Irish Tourist Board), Baggot Street Bridge, Dublin 2 (01) 765871

Bord Bainne (Bord Bainne Co-Operative Ltd), Grattan House, Lower Mount St, Dublin 2 (01) 619599

BIM (Bord Iascaigh Mhara), Hume House, Ballsbridge, Dublin 4 (01) 683956

CERT (CERT Ltd), 1 Ailesbury Road, Dublin 4 (01) 693522

CHALLENGE (CHALLENGE - Equality for Women in Health/Social Welfare and Income Tax Code), 15 Clonard Drive, Dublin 14 (01) 986914

CII (Confederation of Irish Industry), Confederation House, Kildare St, Dublin 2 (01) 779801

Companies Registration Office, Lower Castle Yard, Dame St, Dublin 2 (01) 614222

Commission of the European Communities (Dublin Office), 39 Molesworth St, Dublin 2 (01) 712244

Crafts Council of Ireland Ltd, Thomas Prior House, Merrion Road, Ballsbridge, Dublin 4 (01) 680764

CREW (Centre for Research on European Women), 38 rue Stevin, 1040 Brussels, Belgium (16 32 2) 640 0844

CSW (Council for the Status of Women), 64 Lower Mount St, Dublin 2 (01) 615268/611791

CSO (Central Statistics Office), Earlsfort Terrace, Dublin 2 (01) 767531

CTT (Coras Trachtála - Irish Export Board), Merrion Hall, Strand Road, Sandymount, Dublin 4 (01) 695011

Department of Labour, Burlington Road, Dublin 4 (01) 765861

Department of Social Welfare, 15 Sundrive Road, Dublin 12 (01) 542607

EEA (Employment Equality Agency), 36 Upper Mount St, Dublin 4 (01) 605966/605257

EOLAS (The Irish Science and Technology Agency), Glasnevin, Dublin 9 (01) 370101

Equal Opportunities Office, Service V-A-4, Commission of the European Communities, 200 rue de la Loi, B-1049 Brussels, Belgium

ENOW (European Network of Women), c/o Council for the Status of Women, 64 Lower Mount St, Dublin 2 (01) 615268/611791

FAS (An Foras Aiseanna Saothair - The Training and Employment Authority), 27-33 Upper Baggot St, Dublin 4 (See local directories for local offices)

FUE (The Federated Union of Employers), Baggot Bridge House, 84-86 Lower Baggot St, Dublin 2 (01) 601011

Government Publications Sales Office, Sun Alliance House, Molesworth St, Dublin 2 (01) 710309

ICC (Industrial Credit Corporation), 32 Harcourt St, Dublin 2 (01) 24140; 46 Grand Parade, Cork (021) 277666; 57 O'Connell St, Limerick (061) 317577

ICOS (Irish Co-Operative Organisation Society Ltd), 84 Merrion Square, Dublin 2 (01) 764783/688841

IDA (Industrial Development Authority), Wilton Park House, Wilton Place, Dublin 2 (01) 686633 (See local directories for regional centres)

IMI (Irish Management Institute), Sandyford Road, Dublin 16 (01) 601377

Insurance Corporation of Ireland, Burlington Road, Dublin 4 (01) 601377

Innovation Centre for Small Industry, Plassey Technological Park, Castleroy, Limerick (061) 48177

IPA (Institute of Public Administration), 59 Lansdowne Road, Dublin 4 (01) 686233

IPC (Irish Productivity Centre), 35 Shelbourne Road, Dublin 4 (01) 686244

Irish Exporters Association, Marshalsea House, Merchants Quay, Dublin 8 (01) 770285

IGC (Irish Goods Council), Ireland House Trade Centre, Strand Road, Dublin 4 (01) 696011

Irish Quality Control Association, Shelbourne House, Shelbourne Road, Dublin 4 (01) 683311

MAC (Microelectronics Admissions Centre) University of Limerick, Plassey Technological Park, Castletroy, Limerick (061) 44024)

NETWORK (Organisation for Professional Women) PO Box 1439, Shelbourne Road, Dublin 4 (01) 973386

Network For Women in Business, IDA Enterprise Centre, Pearse Street, Dublin 2

Network on Women in Local Employment Initiatives, c/o Malachy Prunty, ICOS, 84 Merrion Square, Dublin 2 (01) 764783

NISO (National Industrial Safety Organisation) Mespil Road, Dublin 2 (01) 765861

NMRC (National Microelectronics Research Centre) University College, Cork (021) 276871

Patents Office, 45 Merrion Square, Dublin 2 (01) 614144

PMTC (Plassey Management and Technology Centre) University of Limerick, Plassey Technological Park, Limerick (061) 33364

Redwood Ireland Training Association (Assertiveness Courses) 121 Rail Park, Maynooth, Co. Kildare (01) 286482

Regional Technical Colleges, Athlone, Carlow, Cork, Dundalk, Galway, Letterkenny, Sligo, Tralee, Waterford. Contact the principal of the individual colleges for information

Registrar of Business Names, Lower Castle Yard, Dame Street, Dublin 2 (01) 614222

Revenue Commissioners, (Payments to Collector-General) Apollo House, Tara Street, Dublin 2, (01) 716998 (General Administration) St Martin's House, Waterloo Road, Dublin 4 (01) 688666

School of Management Studies, College of Commerce, Rathmines, Dublin 6 (01) 975334

SFADCO (Shannon Free Airport Development Co. Ltd) Shannon Town Centre, Co. Clare (061) 61555

SIPTU (Service, Industrial and Professional Trade Union) Liberty Hall, Dublin 1 (01) 749731

Small Firms Association, Confederation House, Kildare Street, Dublin 2 (01) 779801

SRC (Social Research Centre) University of Limerick, Plassey Technological Park, Limerick (061) 333644

The Irish Federation of Self Employed Ltd, 21 Mespil Road, Dublin 4 (01) 602644

The Marketing Institute of Ireland, 12 Fitzwilliam Place, Dublin 2 (01) 685176

Udarás na Gaeltachta, Na Forbacha, Gaillimh (091) 21011 (check telephone directory for regional centres)

Universities: Limerick, Dublin City University, UCC, UCD, UCG, St, Patrick's College Maynooth, Trinity College, Queen's University, University of Ulster (contact the individual universities for information)

VEC (Vocational Education Committee) (Check telephone directory for local VEC offices)

VAT Administration 4th Floor, 4/5 Harcourt Rd, Dublin 2 (01) 784111

VHI (Voluntary Health Insurance Board) VHI House, 20 lr Abbey Street, Dublin 1 (01) 724499/749171 (check telephone directory for regional offices)

Women's Advisory Committee of ICTU (Irish Congress of Trades Unions) Congress House, 19 Raglan Road, Dublin 4 (01) 680641

Women's Education Bureau, rue de la Loi 200 B-1049, Brussels, Belgium (16 32 2) 235 1111

Where to go for Assistance

Education, Training and Recruitment

Management and Supervisory Training: FAS, IDA, IMI, PMTC, The School of Management Studies, Regional Technical Colleges, EOLAS, Irish Quality Control Association

Operative Training: FAS, IDA, Udarás na Gaeltachta, Vocational Education Committees, Regional Technical Colleges

Sectoral: BIM, CERT, FAS

Recruitment: FAS, Udarás na Gaeltachta

Business Start-up

Identification of Opportunity: IDA, Shannon Development, EOLAS, Innovation Centres (Limerick, Dublin, Galway, Cork), CTT, IGC

Company Formation: Solicitor, Auditor, Companies Registration Office

Insurance: VHI, Insurance Brokers, Insurance Companies

Mergers/Takeovers: ICC, IDA merchant banks

Provision of Factories: IDA, Shannon Development, Udarás na Gaeltachta

Management Advice: IPC Business Advisory Service, Shannon Development, FUE

Assistance, Information and Publications: IDA, Central Statistics Office, Udarás na Gaeltachta, Shannon Development, BIM, EOLAS, IMI, IPC, CTT, CII, FAS, Revenue Commissioners, Department of Labour, Network for Women in Business Representation: CII

Management of Finance

Information and Advice: Auditors, Accountants, the bank, state agencies, IPC and management consultants, chartered surveyors

Financing, Fixed Assets and Working Capital: IDA, Udarás na Gaeltachta, Shannon Development, ICC, commercial banks, financing companies, merchants banks, life assurance companies, private individuals, debt factoring companies, venture capital companies, credit unions, equal opportunities office of the Commission of the EC

Credit-Control: Credit Agencies

Sectoral: BIM, Bord Fáilte, ACC

Management of Production, Marketing and Personnel Information

Advice: EOLAS, Shannon Development, SRC, Network, IPC, IDA

Training: The Marketing Institute of Ireland, IMI, FAS, PMTC

Testing: EOLAS, IDA, Shannon Development, Udarás na Gaeltachta, PMTC

Design and Development: EOLAS, SRC, Innovation Centres, MAC, NMRC

Crafts: Crafts Council of Ireland, IDA

Safety: NISCO

Quality Control: Irish Quality Control Association

Home Market: Irish Goods Council (Forbairt)

Export Markets: CTT, EOLAS, Industrial Credit Corporation, Irish Exporters Association

Personnel: IMI, Department of Labour

Suggested Further Reading

Women and Work

Code of Practice on Equal Opportunity at Work Dublin: Employment Equality Agency
Hodgkinson, L. The Working Woman's Guide, Wellingborough: Thorsons, 1985
Information leaflets on *Women in the Workplace* include:
Employment Equality Act, 1977 (EEA)
Equal Pay (EEA)
Employment Equality Agency (EEA)
Equality at Work (How the EEA Can Help You) (EEA)
Equality at Work (Positive Approaches) (EEA)
Equality at Work (Sexual Harassment) (EEA)
Job Advertising (EEA)
Women's Charter (ICTU)
Guidelines on Sexual Harassment (ICTU)
Positive Action for Equal Opportunities at Work: Guidelines for Negotiations (ICTU)
La Rouche, J. and Ryan, R., *Strategies for Women at Work* London: Counterpoint, 1985
Sharpe, S. *Double Identity: The Lives of Working Mothers* Middlesex: Penguin Books, 1984

Women and Business Start-Up

Birley, S., *New Enterprise: A Start-Up Case Book* London and Canberra: Croom Helm, 1982
Flexman, N. and Scanlan, T., *Running Your Own Business. How to Evaluate and Develop Your Entrepreneurial Skills* Allen, Texas: Argus Communications, 1982
Glascock, S., *A Woman's Guide to Starting Her Own Business* Glasgow: Panther, 1984
IDA, *Your Own Business. A Guide to Setting Up and Running a Small Firm* Dublin: IDA, 1984
Linehan, M., O'Leary, C. and Tucker, V., *How to Start a Co-Op* Cork: Bank of Ireland Centre for Co-Op Studies, UCC, 1981
Prunty, M., *Women in Local Employment Initiatives in Ireland* Dublin: Irish Co-Operative Organisation Society Ltd., 1988
Women Mean Business: An Introduction to Setting Up Your Own Small Business Dublin: Department of Industry and Commerce

Business Management

Cashman, A., *Money Matters for Women* Dublin: Attic Press, 1989
EWMD News, Newsletter of the European Women's Management Development Network
Export Review Coras Trachtála
Export Information Coras Trachtála
MacCormac, M. and Teeling, J., *Financial Management* Dublin: Gill and MacMillan
Records and Bookkeeping In the Small Business Dublin: Irish Banks' Standing Committee, 1984
Winkler, J *Pricing for Results* Dublin: Irish Management Institute in association with W Heinemann Ltd and the Institute of Marketing, 1983

Life-Skills and Stress Management

Baer, J., *How to Be an Assertive (Not Aggressive) Woman in Life, in Love, and on the Job* New York: Signet Books, 1976
Charlesworth, E. and Nathan, R., *Stress Management. A Comprehensive Guide to Your Well-Being* Corgi Books, 1987
Corkille Briggs, D., *Celebrate Your Self. Enhancing Your Own Self Esteem* New York: Doubleday, 1977
O'Connor, J. and Ruddle, H., *You Can Do It! A Life and Work Skills Book for Women* Dublin: Gill and MacMillan, 1989
Phillips, A. and Rakusen, J., *The New Our Bodies Ourselves: A Health Book by and For Women* Middlesex: Penguin Books, 1989

Index

INFORMATION MATTERS
FOR WOMEN

ATTIC HANDBOOKS

SOCIAL WELFARE FOR WOMEN
Sally Keogh and Ita Mangan. 604 £2.95 / $7.95

MONEY MATTERS FOR WOMEN
Aileen Cashman. 752 £3.95 / $7.95

SURVIVING SEXUAL ABUSE
Rosemary Liddy & Deirdre Walsh. 612 £3.95 / $7.95

SEPARATION AND DIVORCE MATTERS FOR WOMEN
Dervla Browne. 884 £3.95 / $7.95

BODY MATTERS FOR WOMEN
Aine McCarthy. 868 £3.95 / $7.95

BUSINESS MATTERS FOR WOMEN
Joyce O'Connor and Helen Ruddle. 876 £4.95 / $ 9.95

SEX EDUCATION AND HEALTH MATTERS FOR GIRLS
Chi Maher. 922 £3.95 / $7.95

PREMENSTRUAL SYNDROME - YOUR OPTIONS
Helen Duckworth. 671 £4.95 / $9.95

EMIGRATION MATTERS FOR WOMEN
Kate Kelly and Triona Nic Giolla Choille. 973 £4.95 / $7.95

For catalogue and mail order inquiries please contact:
Attic Press, 44 East Essex Street, Dublin 2, Ireland.